LIGHT

IN THE

DARKNESS

My Search for Meaning

Greg Wyatt

Published by:
HAVAH Publishing
Ashland, OH
Havahpublishing.com

ISBN: 978-1-64751-026-8

Editor and Interior Layout Design: Amy Rice

Every attempt has been made to source properly all quotes.

Printed in the United States of America

First Edition

WHAT PEOPLE ARE SAYING ABOUT GREG WYATT:

"Every so often you come across a rare breed, one which emits an equally rare light. Greg is bigger than life when, by close examination, you find that his insights and overall meekness sharpens your perspective with laser-like keenness, making you realize you will never be the same. Greg Wyatt is one of my chosen teachers, my brother in Christ, and my forever friend. I am glad he is finally putting his story in print." –J.W.

"Greg has saved me a lot of time with his research and discernment skills. I will forever be appreciate of all the time and effort he puts into bringing the rest of us from darkness into light." –S.C.

"You are courageous and such an inspirational man, Greg. Thank you for all your hard work in exposing the corruption of big pharma. Lots of love from Ireland." –I.E.

"Since I have known him, Greg has been crusading against the things of this world that are harming people. He does not discriminate in his concern and is an inspiration to other truth tellers as we all battle against the darkness. I was able to sneak peek this book, and you want to read it."—E.R.

"Greg is one of the top few that really know what is going on and is willing to step up to the plate to be the mouthpiece of exposing the evil against our children and loved ones. It has been an honor to watch as Greg shares updates on Weston and Emily's lives, opening his life and home for all to see. I am awaiting your books so I can share them with others! This fight takes a toll on the body, but it is not in vain nor are your words falling on deaf ears, I can guarantee that. May we all rise up to be the voice for the children. Love and hugs to you." –F.F.

Dedication:

To my beautiful and talented wife,

My partner, best friend, and the most wonderful mother to our children. You have changed my life and many others in ways you may never realize. You have taught me, inspired me, and stuck with me through thick and thin, for better and worse, for richer and poorer, in sickness and in health, until death do us part. I will love and honor you all the days of my life. You have never once let me down, and I am eternally grateful. You look just as beautiful now as you did in our wedding pictures in March 1995. Thank you for the beautiful years and life.

To my mother and father,

You endured unimaginable hardships to bring me into this world. You guided me down the right path as a young boy and into manhood, despite my own struggles. You never gave up on me. Thank you for

5

always being there, never judging me, and loving me unconditionally. I miss you every day. Not a day goes by where I don't feel your presence within me.

To my dearest sisters, Lisa and Jodi,

You traveled halfway around the world to be part of our family. As a young boy yearning for siblings, God blessed me with two perfect and loving sisters. I am grateful for your presence in my life, today and forever.

To all my friends all around the world,

Thank you for allowing me to be myself and share my life. I hope that my journey teaches you as much as I have learned from yours. Life is no easy road, but together we are making a difference. I look forward to working on the next book to share with you as I finish my journey. Never give up. Never again give in. We have the power to move mountains and change the world.

With love and gratitude,

Greg Wyatt

A letter to my beautiful children, Weston and Emily,

You are the greatest blessings that have been bestowed upon me, filling my days with laughter, warmth, and an abundance of love. Through your presence, you have brought immeasurable happiness and purpose to my life, and for that, I am eternally grateful. Your infectious and radiant smiles pull me through to fight against the agenda that damaged you.

Weston, my son, you are a beacon of strength and resilience. Your determination and unwavering spirit inspire me each day. Your curiosity reminds me of the beauty of learning and growing, despite your intellectual disabilities. I am proud to see you take on new challenges and witness your accomplishments.

May you continue to shine bright and embrace life's adventures with your natural curiosities for the things in life.

Emily, my daughter, you possess a kind and gentle soul that radiates warmth and compassion. Your empathy and thoughtfulness towards others touch the hearts of those around you. I am in awe of your uniqueness and the joy you bring into our lives and the world with your non-stop singing and dancing. May you always embrace your individuality and pursue your dreams with determination.

To all the families who understand our lives through your own experiences, you are the pillars of support, the ones who uplift us during challenging times. My goal has been to be a support for you as well. Your love and unwavering presence have made a profound impact on our journey. We are grateful for the bonds we have formed.

This dedication is a tribute to all the beautiful children and families who brighten our world, with and without disabilities. Our family has been fortunate to receive your love for both of our intellectually disabled children. You are the heart and soul of our lives, and we are blessed to have you by our side. May our connection and love continue to grow, and may we cherish each precious moment we spend together.

(My views do not reflect these quotes, but this book proves their relevance to how humans have been treated through time.)

"It is better for all the world, if instead of waiting to execute degenerate offspring for crime, or to let them starve for their imbecility, society can prevent those who are manifestly unfit from continuing their kind....Three generations of imbeciles are enough."

– U.S. Supreme Court Justice Oliver Wendell Holmes Jr., *Buck v. Bell*, 1927

"Society must concern itself not chiefly with the isolation, temporary or permanent, of the individual murderer, thief, or forger, but with the extermination or repair of the genetic, educational, or industrial defects which cause the production of criminals."

– Charles Eliot, *The New York Times*, December 28, 1915

"Every single case of inherited defect, every malformed child, every congenitally tainted human being brought into this world is of infinite importance to that poor individual; but it is of scarcely less importance to the rest of us and to all of our children who must pay in one way or another for these biological and racial mistakes."

– Margaret Sanger, *The Pivot of Civilization*, 1922 and founder of Planned Parenthood

"The way of nature has always been to slay the hindmost, and there is still no other way, unless we can prevent those who would become the hindmost being born. It is in the sterilization of failures, and not in the selection of successes for breeding, that the possibility of an improvement of the human stock lies."

– H. G. Wells

"The aim of eugenics is to represent each class or sect by its best specimens; that done, to leave them to work out their common civilization in their own way."

– Francis Galton, *Eugenics: Its Definition, Scope, and Aims*, 1904

Contents

Introduction

My story revolves around the pursuit of truth, a universal quest that resonates with us during our time on this Earth. Another significant aspect of my journey is the discovery of forgiveness after uncovering the truth. In our society, facts and information form the foundation of everything, or so we are led to believe. However, there are instances when these facts are disregarded, forgotten, or purposefully altered. Yet, amidst this turmoil, one truth remains unwavering—a truth that I found through my connection with a higher power, an inner faith that guides me.

When contemplating the subversion of truth through lies and deceit, two historical events spring to mind. The first is the Holocaust, which still faces denial from some individuals. This denial is a divisive tactic society employs to conquer and discredit the truth. They twist factual information to such an extent that reality becomes an incredulous falsehood. The second event that comes to mind is the days of Noah, when humanity denied the existence of those days and continued down destructive paths. And here we are again, in a technologically advancing society with a wealth of information available. People are still subverting obvious truths that I have spent my life making available for those with eyes to see and ears to hear.

Regarding my faith, certain intellectuals allow their minds to supersede their hearts, perceiving spirituality as nothing more than a collection of ancient tales. Yet, within our hearts, its significance surpasses such a narrow interpretation. One only needs to observe the world today to understand why our once connected society has become fractured. We have compromised our relationship with our higher power, and that has had profound consequences for our lives and our communities.

One precious gift bestowed upon me is a profound gift of knowledge—an answer to my years of prayer. Once this knowledge is granted, it can never be taken away. With faith, I have seen miraculous shifts in my life, and challenges that seemed insurmountable were cleared from my path.

Through this unwavering faith, I have acquired an ever-expanding gift of knowledge. It seems that the more I embrace my connection with the higher power, the more insights I gain. It is as if the universe responds to the depth of my commitment.

My story commences on June 8th, 1983, my twenty-eighth birthday, in a drug treatment center in Boulder, Colorado. Up until that point, my life had lacked coherence. I was searching for something I couldn't quite grasp, unaware of what it was.

Like countless others, I turned to smoking pot. Our mantra was, "The Vietnam War is a fraud, Nixon is a liar, don't trust anyone over 30, tune in, turn on, drop out." As I delved deeper, I discovered that deception and falsehood permeated every aspect of society. All I yearned for was to unearth the answers I sought. However, alongside these feelings, I sensed a profound imbalance in my life, as if something was terribly wrong. It gnawed at my mind like a relentless rat, a secret and sinister presence embedded in my soul.

I grew up as an only child during the first ten years of my life. Then, on one sweltering summer day, my mother summoned me into the kitchen and posed a question that caught me off guard. She asked me what I thought about having a sister. I was perplexed since she wasn't pregnant, and the idea seemed foreign. The closest thing I had to a sibling was a doll named Renee, a gift my mother had bestowed upon me when I was four years old. Loneliness had been my constant companion, and I always felt out of place.

My mother must have noted the questions stirring silently below the surface because she added, "Well, we'll have to go halfway around the world to get her, and her skin will be brown instead of white. What do you think of that?" With curiosity piqued, I replied after careful thought, "God loves all children!" It was a response that mirrored the Christian values instilled in me by my parents from an early age, even though I was just ten years old.

My mother deeply loved children, which made me wonder why I had grown up as an only child. Furthermore, I pondered why I differed so drastically from my father. I had blonde hair, green eyes, and fair skin, while my father stood short, with thick dark hair and a dark, ruddy complexion. I sensed something was amiss in my heart, and I believed I was adopted.

Observing our humble house, devoid of air conditioning, furnished with hand-me-downs, and a perpetually broken-down car that spent more time in the repair shop than in our driveway, I noticed the contrast with my friends' new clothing. I witnessed my father's arrival home, utterly exhausted, late in the evening after enduring twelve-hour shifts five to six days a week. He would have Saturdays off and Mom would tell him to take me with him as he went around visiting his 'haunts' and the people he knew. My favorite was the 1950's-60's gas stations, with the smell of gas, and the plastic covered calendars that I always managed to sneak a peek of, making breasts a vivid part of my memories of roaming with my dad.

Although we were financially impoverished, we were rich in spirit. In the next eighteen months, not just one but two infant sisters entered our lives, arriving from a distant country called Korea. This decision was a significant leap, considering that the United States was embroiled in a full-scale war with another Asian nation, Vietnam. I witnessed my mother's pioneering spirit and the love she bestowed upon these children as they grew from infancy to adolescence and, ultimately, into adulthood. Racism held no place in our family or neighborhood, even though it pervaded the outside world, or at least I thought so.

And so, on that fateful morning of my twenty-eighth birthday, within the confines of that drug treatment center in Boulder, Colorado, my mother and I, accompanied by my drug counselor, found ourselves behind closed doors, tears mingling with words that would forever alter the course of my life.

She began, "Greg, there is something I must tell you."

Instantly, I leaped from my chair, exclaiming, "I knew it! I'm adopted! You lied to me all these years! I already knew the truth, and yet you never told me," my anger surfacing.

"No, Greg," she responded softly, her voice trailing off. "You are not adopted. I gave birth to you.

You are my son." Her words hung in the air, heavy with emotion. "However, your father is not your biological father. You were conceived through artificial insemination." At that moment, my entire life flashed before my eyes. Everything I had believed, and everything I thought I was, crumbled away. My existence felt counterfeit. I struggled to process this newfound information. A part of me was lost, as if half of my identity had been stolen.

"Mom, who is my biological father?" I inquired, desperately searching her eyes.

She looked down at the floor, fidgeting nervously, grappling for the right words. After a moment of silence, she whispered, "I'm sorry, everything was done in secret, Greg. And all those years, I kept it silent because I thought telling the truth was a crime. I didn't want to be arrested. I'm so sorry. There's just no way you will ever be able to find that information out.."

Another question rolled out of my mouth. "Why couldn't Dad have children? Why couldn't he have been my biological father?"

Putting on a stoic face to offset the information rolling from her tongue, she spilled that as a young boy, during the Great Depression of the 1930s, the man I had spent a lifetime believing was my father had been placed in the Beatrice State Home for feeble-minded youth, which was actually a social dumping ground for the poor and unwanted people of society. These state homes were like concentration camps, work farms. It was no secret that back then, if you had too many mouths to feed or a child giving you trouble, you could take them down to the Beatrice State Home for Feeble-Minded Youth, pay them $75, and they would be out of your life for good. Forever. While Hitler had his concentration camp for the Jews in the 1930s and 40s during World War II, even before that, the United States of America had their own type of concentration camps, which operated as work farms, for the poor, troublemakers, petty criminals, unloved, and the unwanted. If, for any reason, you would be fortunate enough to be released as part of your release agreement, it was mandatory that you be sterilized so that, genetically speaking, you would never produce another inferior offspring of your kind. While the words she used were different, and the sentiment is mine, (you get the picture).

The revelation struck me like a thunderbolt. I was consumed by a profound sense of loss, abandonment, and a burning desire to uncover the truth. Questions swirled in my mind like a tempestuous storm. Who was my biological father? Why was I conceived through artificial insemination? Why had I been kept in the dark all these years?

I realized that my search for truth had taken on a whole new dimension at that moment. I was no longer solely seeking answers about the world's deceit and deception, but I was now embarking on a deeply personal quest to uncover the truth about my origins.

With the support of loved ones and a newfound resilience, I embarked on a tireless quest to unearth the truth. I delved into the depths of my mother's past, searching for any clue that could lead me closer to the identity of my biological father. I combed through faded photographs, old letters, and fragments of conversations, piecing together details of a puzzle long kept hidden.

As I dug deeper, the picture slowly began to take shape. I discovered whispers of a name, fragments of stories, and a trail that led me to distant lands. The journey became more than a mere pursuit of genetic information; it became a quest for self-discovery and acceptance.

Along the way, I encountered resistance and roadblocks. Some family members were reluctant to share their secrets, while others had simply vanished into the mists of time. But I refused to be deterred. I sought out distant relatives, combed through ancestral records, and reached out to individuals who might hold a missing piece of the puzzle.

Through the process, I came face to face with the darker side of humanity—the pain, betrayal, and hidden truths beneath the surface. The parallels between my personal quest and the societal quest for truth became strikingly apparent. I witnessed firsthand the power of deception and the lengths people would go to protect their secrets.

But amidst the shadows, I also encountered glimmers of hope and acts of compassion. Strangers became allies, extending a helping hand when I needed it most. I learned that even in the darkest corners, some are willing to shine a light and offer support on the path to truth.

Through it all, I held onto faith—a faith that transcended religious dogma and embraced the belief that truth, in its purest form, is a beacon that guides us toward healing and liberation. I found solace in the words of Jesus, who proclaimed, "The truth shall set you free." This truth became my guiding star, a constant reminder of the importance of staying steadfast in my pursuit, regardless of the challenges ahead.

And so, my story continues—an odyssey of self-discovery, forgiveness, and redemption. It is a testament to the resilience of the human spirit and the unwavering desire to unravel the mysteries that shape our lives. With each step forward, I come closer to embracing my true identity, no longer defined solely by biology but by the strength and courage that have propelled me on this extraordinary journey.

A light has emerged in the depths of darkness—an unwavering beacon illuminating the path toward my own truth. And as I navigate the twists and turns of this intricate tapestry, I am reminded that the search for truth is not confined to external forces but resides within the depths of our hearts. It is a journey we all undertake to understand our place in this vast universe and find meaning amidst the chaos.

And so, I press on, fueled by a light that refuses to be extinguished, a light that beckons me forward, guiding me through the darkness and reminding me that in the pursuit of truth, there is always the possibility of finding redemption and a renewed sense of purpose.

Chapter 1

Baby Boom:

Seeds of Hope

Let me take you back to September 8, 1954, a sweltering day in Lincoln, Nebraska. The atmosphere was thick with humidity as the events of that day unfolded, mirroring the weight of the decisions being made behind closed doors.

In a small and modest doctor's office, Betty, my mother, made a decision that would change the course of her life. With determination and a touch of nervousness, she signed a consent form. Little did she know that this moment would mark the beginning of a remarkable journey that would not be possible any other way.

The room was adorned with a paper-covered physician's table, and as she lay down, her body vulnerable, Betty tried to find comfort in the words of Dr. Thierstein.

"Just relax, Betty," Dr. Thierstein

comforted calmly and reassuringly. "Everything will work out fine. No one needs to know except you, your husband, and me. You're a very fertile woman, and many times this works the first time. Now, relax this will be over in a moment."

The hope of conceiving a child burned brightly within her, and Dr. Thierstein, aware of her fertility, tied his bedside manner to the promise that this procedure might be the key.

Meanwhile, just an hour earlier, a young Dutch student, aged 32, performed a solitary act in a different room. He filled a clear plastic cup with his contribution, unaware of the lives he was unknowingly helping to create. He would forever remain a distant figure, absent from the lives he played a role in creating.

With closed eyes, Betty braced herself as the anonymous sperm was gently introduced into her body through a plastic syringe. The procedure was swift, over in mere seconds. Leaving the doctor's office, Betty's husband, Herbert, opened the car door for her, his actions a testament to their enduring partnership. They embarked on a journey across town in their cherished 1949 Ford coupe, their thoughts consumed by the potential life growing within Betty. Looking out the window, she couldn't help but notice children playing happily in front of rows upon rows of homes.

At that moment, Betty's prayer rose up, a plea to the heavens, begging for the fulfillment of their deepest desire to become parents. "Dear Lord, if it is within your will, let us conceive this special child. You know we would be good parents, and we want a family so bad." It was a prayer she had prayed hundreds of times for the last six years. The weight of six childless years hung heavy in her heart, but a glimmer of hope shone through her tears. Unbeknownst to Betty, the child she was praying for would pray this same prayer with his future wife before receiving their two blessings, years down the line.

Reaching out to her husband, she placed her trembling hand on his knee, silently acknowledging their shared longing. Herbert, unable to meet her gaze, felt a tear escape his eye. She was not the infertile one, and as a man, the stress of his failure was stifling, even if the cause had been outside his control.

That night, Betty and Herb made love, their union a symbol of their faith in the child they had yet to meet. It was an intimate moment that belonged solely to them, a memory they would cherish forever. This night held the promise of a future only they could imagine, a secret bond between two souls.

The following day, life in the Wyatt household resumed its normal rhythm. Herbert dutifully dedicated 60 hours, or more, each week to his minimum wage job, his tireless work a testament to his unwavering commitment to his wife. Rising before the break of dawn, he left out the door by six in the morning, only returning when twelve hours had passed. He returned each evening, fatigue etched on his face, his calloused hands clutching a worn-out aluminum lunchbox and a silver hard hat bearing his nickname, "Shorty." Six days each week, this was his routine.

Standing at a compact height of 5'2", his muscular frame bore the marks of sun-kissed skin, a testament to his unwavering dedication to providing for his family. To ensure Betty's convenience during the day, he relied on a coworker's generosity, who provided transportation to and from work. Herbert took pride in his role as a provider, tirelessly laboring to bring home a modest paycheck each week. Their commitment to planning for the future was evident as they diligently saved money in a small account at the local Havelock bank. They acknowledged the importance of preparing for unforeseen circumstances in post-war America, a time of flourishing opportunities.

Weeks passed swiftly, and Betty's anticipation grew with each passing day. Her period was several days overdue, a subtle yet promising sign. With her heart pounding in her chest, she picked up the phone and dialed the number of Dr. Thierstein's office. Determined to uncover the truth, she sped down the streets, her mind racing with excitement and anxiety. Pulling up to the doctor's office, she took a moment to freshen up her red lipstick, stealing a glimpse of her reflection in the rearview mirror. She realized the magnitude of the moment that awaited her in that instant.

Betty parked her car outside the doctor's office, barely avoiding the curb. She quickly glanced at her rearview mirror, ensuring her tears hadn't ruined her makeup. Taking a deep breath, she looked up and whispered a prayer, her heart yearning for what she desired most—to become a mother. "Dear God, all I've ever wanted was to be a mom. Please, Lord, grant me this opportunity. I promise I won't let you down." As Betty stepped out of the shiny black coupe, a surge of longing swept through her. She wished Herbert could be by her side, sharing this nerve-wracking yet pivotal moment.

With renewed hope, Betty hurried into the waiting room, announcing her presence and finding a seat. Despite her anticipation, she remained calm while waiting for her name to be called.

Before long, she sat in Dr. Thierstein's office, surrounded by his numerous awards and accolades. The walls displayed the remarkable achievements of his career, instilling a sense of confidence and trust.

Dr. Thierstein performed what was known as a frog test, a pregnancy test of the time. Within moments, the examination revealed a positive result, bringing forth a smile of pride upon the doctor's face.

"Well, Betty, you're pregnant," he exclaimed, peering over his wire-rimmed glasses. His words carried a mix of joy and assurance.

"Your baby is due to enter the world on June 8, 1955—almost nine months from the day of your insemination."

Chapter 2

Genetic Bewilderment:

Like Father, Like Son

I sensed something was amiss in our family dynamics from an early age. My parents were of small stature, with my father standing at a mere 5'2", the same height as my mother. They weighed less than 130 pounds at their peak, while I surpassed them in size at the tender age of 12. My blonde hair sharply contrasted with my father's thick, dark locks, and his weathered complexion bore witness to countless hours of toiling under the scorching sun.

As I grew up, our differences became even more apparent. Silently, I would observe his mannerisms and feel disconnected from him. While some of my discontent is recognized in hindsight, the unvoiced thoughts and ignored feelings are no less real now than they were then. I vividly recall gazing at my father on the couch, the blaring

television serving as background noise while he dozed off with his mouth agape. I would sit there, fixated on him for extended periods, unable to fathom how he could be my father. The simplest of similarities would allow me to convince myself, "Like father, like son. Our genetics must've gotten jumbled somewhere, but this thing I noticed proves we're one and the same."

Returning home at night, he would collapse on the couch, exhausted, an open newspaper resting on his chest. Little did I know then, but he was illiterate and unable to read.

Our meals consisted mainly of my mother's cooking, from scratch. However, they typically revolved around the same theme: meat and potatoes prepared in countless variations. The house perpetually smelled like a bakery, as my mother loved baking. She tried her best, pouring her heart into each dish. In hindsight, I would give her an "A" for effort, but back then, as a rebellious renegade, I failed to appreciate much beyond my limited existence. The weight of confusion overwhelmed me.

Upon graduating high school, I deliberately entered the workforce instead of pursuing a college education. Part of my rationale stemmed from the belief that I was intellectually superior to my peers. My mind turning over and questioning the need for a mere piece of paper. The second reason echoed the sentiment of "like father, like son." I deeply respected that saying, and I didn't want to surpass my father by becoming something more than he was. I wanted to be like him. So, after high school, I took on numerous jobs in the labor market—working in a foundry, a manufacturing plant, and even as a garbage collector.

The list continued, consisting of menial jobs that appeared to offer limited prospects for the future.

The neighborhood was aptly named Havelock, a blue-collar neighborhood made up mostly of Burlington Northern railroaders and other blue-collar workers from the various other manufacturing facilities that provided good jobs and stable incomes. There was a main street, Havelock Avenue, with hardware and grocery stores, mom and pop restaurants with the tastiest food you can find, banks, shoe stores, a pharmacy, clothing stores, etc. Businesses clustered in buildings that were built between 1900 and 1920, typical of many small towns. There was nothing missing from Havelock.

Our house lacked air conditioning, and fans ran incessantly day and night, attempting to combat the stifling heat of Nebraska's hot and humid summers. I used the profits from my marijuana endeavors to acquire things my parents could never afford. One such luxury was an air conditioner, making my room the only oasis of coolness in our home.

And so, during the years spanning from 1972 to 1976, confusion marked a significant season in my life. As I matured and entered my twenties, my perception of many things underwent a profound transformation, and with it, my bewilderment intensified.

Chapter 3

Finally, the Truth:

Wrestling with Uncertainty

It was the spring of 1983 when I stumbled upon the truth about my conception. I was a successful car salesman at that time, living a life filled with parties and excess. My friend and fellow salesman, Dan, who battled addiction, found himself in a rehab center in Boulder, Colorado. Concerned for his well-being, I visited him to see how he was doing.

As I stood in front of the mirror that night, snorting cocaine, I realized my life had become chaotic. The lines of white powder blurred together, and a sense of disorientation washed over me. In a moment of clarity, I flushed the remaining white powder down the toilet and pleaded with God to help me escape this destructive path.

The next day, I drove to Boulder and committed myself to the rehab center. It was a structured and focused program that aimed to guide individuals toward recovery. Every week, they held a family day where loved ones could participate in the program alongside the patients. As fate would have it, my mother, Betty, decided to join me on June 8th, 1983, which also happened to be my 28th birthday.

That morning, there was a knock on my door, and I was led to a small room with padded chairs and couches. Sitting there was my mother, wearing a bright smile. "Happy birthday, Greg," she greeted me.

We exchanged pleasantries, but beneath the surface, something heavy loomed.

Time passed, and a moment arrived when my counselor, who was present in the room, prompted my mother to speak. With tears in her eyes, she reached out and placed her hand on my knee. The counselor encouraged her to continue. "Greg, there's something I need to tell you," she began.

Overwhelmed by anger and confusion, I blurted out, "I knew it! I'm adopted, and you've lied to me all these years." I could see the shock on my mother's face, but it wasn't a surprise—it was a recognition of my strong intuition.

She tried to clarify, assuring me that I wasn't adopted and was indeed her biological son. However, she disclosed that the man I had believed to be my father was not my biological father. My mind spun with disbelief. How could this be? I wondered if she had an affair, seeking answers to fill the void.

Surprisingly, she revealed that she had undergone artificial insemination using a sperm donor. I pressed further, demanding to know who my father was. But she explained that it was impossible for me to ever find out, as the conception had been shrouded in secrecy. Those involved were strictly instructed to never disclose the truth to anyone.

At that moment, my life felt like a bewildering mix of a thrilling Disneyland ride and the perplexing uncertainty of the Twilight Zone. I struggled to comprehend the enormity of the revelation. Nothing made sense, adding to the confusion that plagued me throughout my life.

After completing a 30-day treatment program, I was released, but my mind remained addicted to new thoughts of my identity—or rather, the lack thereof. I managed to stay sober for a couple of months, but eventually, the demons of my past resurfaced, and I found myself falling back into old patterns.

The obsession with my true identity consumed me, and no matter how hard I tried, I couldn't shake the constant questions and uncertainties. Every face I saw on the street sparked curiosity—could we be related? Were they my brothers, sisters, or even my father? It became a continuous and tormenting presence, making it increasingly difficult to find peace of mind, the world a surreal tapestry of confusion.

Chapter 4

A Stolen Childhood:
Abandoned in Beatrice

Ed and Sadie Foster resided in a dilapidated and impoverished section of Lincoln, Nebraska, known as South Bottoms, alongside their five children: Dick, Dan, Don, Little Herb, and their sister Norma. Their biological father was a chronic alcoholic and negligent parent who prioritized carousing and drunkenness over providing for his family.

One day, he vanished without a trace, leaving Sadie and her children in a tragic predicament. Following the recommendation of a neighbor, Sadie met Ed Foster, another local drunkard with dubious intentions. They quickly married, and from that point onward, things spiraled downward rapidly.

Ed Foster would start drinking from when he woke up until he passed out in the afternoon. This created a torturous hell for the children, who did their best to avoid him at all costs. Conversely, Sadie was a devoted mother who loved her children dearly and feared losing them, as many of her friends had experienced having their kids taken away by the county.

This period coincided with the late 1920s and early 1930s, the onset of the Great Depression. Money was scarce, employment opportunities were scarce, and food was even scarcer, particularly for a family of seven. It was only a matter of time before the terrifying beatings began, continuing almost incessantly.

On a fateful Friday morning, young Herbert Wyatt's life was about to undergo an unimaginable transformation. Ed Foster, Herb's stepfather, took a swig from his flask and discreetly stowed it beneath the car seat. Nervously, he lit his third cigarette, holding it between his crooked yellow teeth as he glanced in the rearview mirror, checking if anyone was following them.

His gaze shifted to the young boy sitting in the backseat—Herb. He had told Herb they were visiting his older brother Richard at the hospital, creating excitement in Herb since he hadn't seen his brother in years. Ed Foster had done this before, and he had similar plans in mind.

Beatrice, Nebraska, located 43 miles south of Lincoln, amidst rolling hills and fertile farmland along the banks of the Big Blue River, served as the backdrop for the events about to unfold. The old, rusty car lurched forward before abruptly coming to a halt.

Three years prior, Ed Foster had taken Herb's brother, Richard, to the Beatrice State Home, paying them $75 and surrendering guardianship. Now, he was repeating the same cruel act with Herb.

Taking Herb's hand, Ed guided him up the granite steps and into the main reception area. Almost instantly, two sturdy orderlies appeared, placing their hands on Herb's shoulders and leading him down the hallway. Little did anyone know that Herb would remain unseen for 14 years.

Within minutes, Herb grasped the grim reality of his situation. His worst nightmare had just begun. Hastily processed, he was taken to another building where numerous other young boys, who had suffered a similar fate, were gathered. It was the depths of the Great Depression, and many parents could not provide adequately for their children and families. Overwhelmed, Herb glanced around with teary eyes, bewildered by the events of the past 90 minutes.

After a short while, Herb was assigned a uniform and shown to his new bed. As the hour grew late, the setting sun signaled lights out, and precisely at 9:00 p.m., the wailing sirens echoed in the background, plunging the room into darkness.

Little Herb tossed and turned on his hard cot throughout the night, accompanied by the other children's crying and whimpering. His mind raced incessantly, yearning for his dog, his mother, but most of all, for his friends. Only managing a couple hours of sleep, Herb awoke as the sun rose over the ridge, the sirens blaring to signal the start of another day.

The children dressed and stood at attention, lined up like toy soldiers readying for war. An orderly entered the room, clutching a clipboard and calling out names. There were 24 children in that ward, and it was a Saturday—a workday, as Sundays were reserved for church in the morning and activities in the afternoon.

Herb was assigned to work in the fields, joining a crew of 12 older boys, his peers in this laborious journey.

Chapter 5

Confronting Government-Imposed Sterilization AKA Eugenics

My father, Herb 'Shorty' Wyatt, was born on September 16th, 1924, into a profoundly impoverished family in Lincoln, Nebraska. His father struggled with alcoholism, and his mother did her best to raise their five children. In the 1930s, it was common for families to place children into state-run institutions when they couldn't afford to care for the children or didn't want too many mouths to feed. They would pay a fee, usually around $75, and sign away their custody rights, effectively separating themselves from their children forever.

One such institution was the Beatrice Institution for Feeble-Minded Youth, a dumping ground for these distressing situations. The May 2nd, 1927, 8-1 Supreme Court ruling in Buck v. Bell provided a legal framework for state enforced sterilizations. This ruling allowed the United States government, through the federal court system, to enact state laws that empowered states and counties to remove children and even parents if they were deemed unfit. These children would then be placed in state-run work farms, where they would endure mandatory labor for the rest of their lives. Many of these institutions were located in smaller towns throughout the Midwest, East Coast, and even some on the West Coast.

Most governments eagerly welcomed this opportunity to obtain free labor and reap substantial

41

profits. In the 1940s, many of these institutions were engaged in producing munitions and war-related parts to support World War II, and they sought inexpensive labor to meet the high demands. If Shorty wasn't working at the munitions plant, he would be assigned tasks in the livestock area or farm fields. The Beatrice State Home was self-sufficient, keeping him occupied with various responsibilities. The home justified the 'residents' working for free since they provided 'free' room and board.

From 1934 to 1949, the Beatrice State Home was Shorty's residence. His whereabouts remained unknown to his family until his brother, Dan, returned home from military service on leave and inquired about his younger brother's whereabouts. In his drunken state, Ed Foster revealed to Dan that Shorty was confined at the Beatrice State Home along with their other brother, Dick. Shocked and horrified, Dan immediately drove to the institution, demanding answers and his younger brother's release. When Dan asked Shorty how he ended up in the institution, Shorty shared a distressing story, mentioning that if he didn't escape soon, he feared he would lose his sanity.

To secure his release, Shorty had to be placed under the care of a family member and put on 'parole,' which is what they called release. Dan agreed to take responsibility. However, the state imposed one condition: Shorty had to undergo sterilization, a procedure intended to prevent him from ever becoming a father and potentially producing what they considered defective offspring.

The day before his release in April 1949, Shorty was awakened by a knock on the door. Outside stood

42

four robust men in white medical jackets. They motioned for him to accompany them and led him down a stark hallway into an operating room. Despite knowing what awaited him, Shorty saw it as a necessary sacrifice for his freedom after enduring all those years of mandatory work and separation from society. Within moments, it was over, and the next day he was finally released at 25 years old.

44

Chapter 6

A Patchwork Family:

Loving Adopted Sisters

My mother possessed an unwavering desire to channel her nurturing instincts toward a larger brood of children. She believed her life would be incomplete without a house bustling with laughter, love, and the pitter-patter of little feet. As I grew older, I began questioning why she and my father couldn't provide me with a sibling, especially considering I was living proof of their capability to conceive. However, the truth surrounding my conception remained concealed, leaving me in a state of yearning that seemed to surpass even my mother's longing for more children to complete our family.

The longing within my mother was palpable, an unquenchable desire that fueled her dreams of a larger household. I could sense the unspoken yearning in her eyes, how she would watch other families with multiple children and ache for a similar experience. She yearned to extend her love, devotion, and care to another child, create lasting bonds. She cherished the joys of raising a family. It was a yearning that surpassed the ordinary, as if her soul yearned for completeness through the presence of additional children. It was a source of contention between her and my father that I was too young to have entirely picked up on, though in hindsight, it becomes abundantly clear.

As a child, I couldn't fathom why my parents hadn't fulfilled my longing for a sibling. After all, I was living evidence of their ability to conceive and raise a child. The question would occasionally escape my lips, innocent and curious, wondering why my house wasn't filled with the laughter and commotion accompanying brothers and sisters. The information that could have provided clarity to my questions was withheld, leaving me in a state of perpetual longing. My yearning for a sibling seemed to grow exponentially, surpassing even the depths of my mother's desire. It was as if my subconscious knew that there was a missing piece to the puzzle of my existence, a piece that held the key to unlocking the sibling bond I so desperately craved.

The disparity between my unfulfilled longing and my mother's unspoken dreams became more pronounced each day. I could see the glimmers of sadness in her eyes, the hidden sighs that escaped her lips when she thought no one was listening. As a result, my mom became a foster parent to numerous children who would stay with us for a few weeks, months, or sometimes even longer. However, it was always agonizing when they were taken away. I consciously tried not to grow too attached, knowing they would eventually leave. The foster care system and these children's constant comings and goings were too complex for me to comprehend at such a young age. What was originally very exciting became a source of unnecessary pain, so I became detached from the process. These were not siblings I would get to keep; they were temporary playmates that liked to capture and take pieces of our hearts with them, leaving the widening gap of instability within our walls.

During this period, my mother started exploring the possibility of adoption. We underwent various evaluations, including child studies and home assessments. However, I didn't know until later that the county would not allow us to adopt white children. They held my father's sterilization and time at the Beatrice State Home for Feeble-Minded Youth against him, deeming him unfit to adopt white children. Strangely enough, they would have allowed us to adopt children of other races. This injustice deeply bothered me, igniting distrust and resentment towards the government, even though I didn't fully grasp the extent of their actions at the time. The financial commitment of adoption was more weight placed on my father's overworked and underappreciated shoulders. He didn't complain. He did everything within his power to make our home and lives what Mom wanted. His love knew no physical boundaries—60 hours of backbreaking work each week turned into 70 when he was putting in overtime, not counting commutes.

Fortunately, everything eventually fell into place, but it wasn't without causing me considerable confusion and angst. I struggled with genetic bewilderment, the inability to fully understand and unravel my identity, all while being clueless about why I would feel that way. It felt as though I was starting life with a disadvantage or handicap imposed upon me from the very beginning.

My mother was an incredibly devoted parent who cherished her children, so this isn't the Freudian tale of early childhood mommy issues. There was no competition for my mother's heart—there was room enough for her genetic son and her adopted daughters. There was never any favoritism. She saw each of us as an answer to specific prayers that existed between her and God alone. In fact, mom did all the 'obnoxious' doting mother—things that society jokes about. She would often dress my sisters in matching outfits, just like Joyce would dress Weston and Emily alike.

My father adored my sisters just as much as he loved me; they were Daddy's girls. He took great pride in our family, regardless of its unconventional composition. I used to refer to us as a patchwork family, pieced together from various corners of the world. This was long before political

correctness and during a war with people that looked like my sisters.

My sisters, Lisa and Jody, knew they were not genetically related to Betty and Herb. No lies or deception were involved, though it would have been harder to keep that genetic secret. Lisa and Jody harbored appreciation and love for all of us. There was no resentment for their lot in life, only gratitude. For the meantime, I had no knowledge that Herb was not my biological father, yet my life felt incomplete and lacked clarity.

Interestingly, Lisa and Jody are not interested in finding their birth parents. They can do so through services like 23andMe or Ancestry, but they simply don't care because Mom and Dad were their actual parents. Being truthful and honest has shaped their perspective, fostering a deep sense of belonging and identity.

Lisa and Jody are entirely different in their personalities, yet they share an incredibly close bond to this day. Sadly, Lisa and I have grown somewhat apart as we've gotten older, but that doesn't take away from the love I have for her. However, my younger sister, Jody, remains as sweet as ever and never forgets a birthday. Both love me unconditionally and immensely, which holds great significance in my heart, even if our contact is not as frequent as I would like, especially in my old age. This is a typical occurrence in America nowadays, where people are geographically distant, and the sense of togetherness has diminished. I will never stop being grateful for both Lisa and Jody! They are miracles, and I am better for them having been added to our family.

The details of our story are documented in a newspaper article from 1968, providing specific dates and capturing the profound impact that my mother, father, and I faced upon welcoming these little girls into our lives. They brought about changes that we could have never imagined or planned

An Armful Of Sugar And Spice

It isn't every young man who can acquire a double portion of "sugar and spice and everything nice" within a year, but far from scorning his little "sisters" (as we imagine most 13 year-old boys do), Gregory Wiatt is as pleased and proud as his parents are to have two sparkling bits of femininity added to the family.

Lisa Sue (at left) is 2½ years-old and arrived from Korea in the spring of 1967 to become the daughter of Mr. and Mrs. Herbert Wiatt. Ten month-old Jodi Lea came from Korea in June to round out the busy household where dolls and "girl talk" have taken their place with bats and balls and "boy talk".

Television, incidentally, played a large part in Lisa's and Jodi's trips to America. Mrs. Wiatt, who confesses she always thought it would be fun to have a little girl in the house, was keeping one eye on the television one morning while doing housework and a program on the Holt Agency and its efforts to provide good homes for Korean-American orphans did the trick. The Wiatt threesome is now the Wiatt fivesome.

Madam Chairman

MORNING
City recreation, children's art, 10 o'clock, Center II.
Nebraska State Medical Auxiliary, board meeting, 9:30 o'clock, Hotel Cornhusker.
Camp Fire Girls, knitting class, 8:45 o'clock, Gold's.
AFTERNOON
Lincoln Woman's Club, Bible department project luncheon, noon at the club house.
EVENING
Lincoln Duplicate Bridge Club, 7:30 o'clock at 2738 South St.

for and every day was worth it. I instantly became the protective and doting older brother, filled with awe and love for my sisters.

[For easier reading, the text in *The Lincoln Star* article says:

Title: "An Armful Of Sugar and Spice (Friday, August 9, 1968)

51

"It isn't every young man who can acquire a double portion of 'sugar and spice and everything nice' within a year, but far from scorning his little 'sisters' (as we imagine most 13-year-old boys do), Gregory W. is as pleased and proud as his parents are to have two sparkling bits of femininity to added to the family.

Lisa Sue (at left) is 2 ½ years old and arrived from Korea in the spring of 1967 to become the daughter of Mr. and Mrs. Herbert W. Ten-month-old Jodi Lee came from Korea in June to round out the busy household where dolls and 'girl talk' have taken their place with bats and balls and 'boy talk.'

Television, incidentally, played a large part in Lisa's and Jodi's trips to America. Mrs. W., who confesses she always thought it would be fun to have a little girl in the house, was keeping one eye on the television one morning while doing housework and a program on the Holt Agency and its efforts to provide good homes for Korean-American orphans did the trick. The W. threesome is now the W. fivesome."]

Chapter 7

My Entrepreneurial Journey:

From a Determined 9-Year-Old to Digital Sales and Marketing

My journey into business began at the age of 9. I witnessed my father, a hardworking laborer, toil for long hours with little to show for it. Despite his dedication, his earnings only provided the basic necessities of food, shelter, and clothing. I couldn't help but feel that there was something more out there.

Growing up in a modest neighborhood in Lincoln, Nebraska, I was unaware of the extent of our poverty. It seemed like everyone lived a similar lifestyle. However, I always yearned for the finer things in life, like candy, enjoyable activities such as bowling and pinball, and even a bicycle, despite not knowing how to ride one at first. Surprisingly, I quickly mastered it, much like other aspects of life that seemed to come effortlessly to me. As a child in the 1960s, simple pleasures like playing pinball and reading comic books held great significance.

Driven by my desire for independence and a few extra cents, I discovered a way to earn money by collecting discarded pop bottles, each worth a penny. I created my own small recycling route, scouring the neighborhood and accumulating 10 to 20 bottles every few days. I would then trade them in at the store for candy. Eventually, I outgrew this venture and began spending more money on my growing interests.

Riding my bicycle provided me with a sense of freedom, allowing me to escape the tense atmosphere at home, filled with constant bickering between my parents. They would fight about money; there never seemed to be enough. It was during one of my rides through the neighborhood that I stumbled upon a sign advertising nightcrawlers for sale at 25 cents per dozen. Intrigued by the potential profits, my ever-inquiring mind and entrepreneurial spirit kicked in, and I wondered how much the seller was actually making. This encounter took place around 1967 when I was approximately 12 years old.

Fearlessly, I approached the seller's door, a black man and longtime friend of my father's, knowing deep down what I aimed to achieve—gaining valuable insights, as I still do today. I knew he would answer my inquiries. The door opened, revealing a familiar face. I expressed my curiosity and eagerness to learn more about his business. Unbeknownst to him, I was not simply seeking information; I wanted to emulate his success—a lesson I had learned early on in my sales, marketing, and coaching endeavors, which would come 20 years later.

I inquired about his sales figures, and he shared that on a good day, he could sell 8 to 12 dozen nightcrawlers, earning him three to four dollars. It struck me as far more lucrative than the 20 to 30 cents I earned through hard work collecting pop bottles. I further probed, asking where he obtained the worms. With a glimmer in his eye, he revealed that they were abundant everywhere, especially in the moonlit backyard. Intrigued, I ventured into my own backyard that night, armed with a flashlight, and to my astonishment, thousands of worms lay scattered on the ground. I had discovered a proverbial gold mine.

Motivated by this discovery, I grabbed a coffee can and filled it with coffee grounds, embarking on my first night of worm farming. In just one night, I collected over 100 nightcrawlers. The following day, armed with a makeshift sign, a board, and a stake, I set up a worm-selling operation in our front yard. It didn't take long before my first customer arrived, purchasing a dozen worms for 25 cents. At that moment, I realized I had found a way to create wealth seemingly out of thin air, although it required hard work—a quality lacking in most people and the essential element of successful entrepreneurship.

I had discovered a prime location where thousands of cars passed by each day, heading to various destinations, including a group of fishing lakes located outside of town. The potential for selling worms in that area intrigued me, and I wanted to explore ways to increase my nightcrawler supply and generate even more sales while minimizing my effort. So, I decided to seek guidance from my neighbor, sharing my experiences and expressing my need for more worms.

Curious to learn his secrets, I asked him for advice. He revealed that the best time to collect nightcrawlers was around 9:00 p.m. Armed with a dim flashlight, I would shine it at the ground, and the nightcrawlers would glisten in the moonlight. The key was to act swiftly but with caution, ensuring I didn't break them while grabbing them. I learned to gently hold them, allowing them to relax and then carefully ease them out of their homes. As a young and observant student, I always sought to understand their behavior and find ways to improve my techniques.

Continuing with my entrepreneurial endeavors, I supplemented my income during the hot summer months, and the days were as hot in summer as they were cold in winter, by door-to-door selling all occasion cards. The weather was never an impediment to my sales work. I was accustomed to it. Additionally, I ventured into selling YMCA thin mints and excelled in both ventures. These experiences occurred between the ages of 9 and 13, spanning from 1965 to 1968. The entrepreneurial bug had firmly taken hold of me during that time.

Subsequently, I initiated a lawn mowing service, and my dedicated father would assist me after his grueling 12-hour workdays. He would do anything to support his son. Together, we charged an average of 50 cents per lawn, offering our services to the neighborhood. I quickly discovered my knack for sales and marketing, and it became evident that I had a natural talent for connecting with people. By the time I turned 12, I had accumulated four income opportunities, outearning all my friends. It was like having a full-time job.

Over the following decade, I ventured into various small businesses, and each time, I found success in sales and marketing. It was ingrained in my DNA.

In the 1990s, during the pre-internet era, I seized an opportunity to collaborate with the local trash company and promote recycling. With my company, Recycle America, I developed a door-to-door marketing strategy to win over businesses from multinational trash companies, redirecting their business to local trash and recycling companies. I honed the door-to-door program, quickly assembling a team of a dozen employees. My role shifted to processing paperwork and collecting checks as the business flourished. It was a lucrative gold mine. Eventually, I worked myself out of a job when the next trash company I worked for resold the customers I had acquired from the big trash companies for millions of dollars. I found myself momentarily without a job, but my efforts had made someone else a millionaire.

Deciding to retire at 40, my wife and I relocated to Arizona. She was still running her video stores and was very successful and respected as a businesswoman remotely running several large businesses. We had just brought Weston home, so we were trying to step away from business to focus on our new roles as parents.

Amidst the Y2K concerns, I stumbled upon an incredible opportunity in the dehydrated, freeze-dried, and storable food industry. From a makeshift office in my basement in 1998, I transformed my company, EmergencyFoodStorage.com, into a thriving enterprise with over 20 employees and a 5,000-square-foot warehouse within 90 days. Profits soared, with daily earnings ranging from $5,000 to over $40,000 at its peak.

In the early 2000s, I ventured into real estate, obtaining my salesman's license. However, I quickly realized that the Internet was poised to revolutionize the industry, transforming transactional processes and lead generation. Determined to adapt, I dedicated six months to perfecting my system and becoming Prescott, Arizona's number one online agent. I generated 100 buyer leads per week, which I referred to other agents in my office, taking a 50% cut. I usually had 20 homes in escrow, on average, before the market slowed down and crashed in 2006 to 2008. A lender bought the home buyer leads and I was able to make money hand over fist for the effort I was putting into my work.

Soon, I developed a marketing program for agents and brokers, teaching them how to generate internet leads. The success of my program attracted agents from across the United States, and my local real estate company became the top small brokerage in the area, with over 20 agents and $33 million in sales in our first year. This was a remarkable feat considering the average home price was under $200,000. My lead generation system was voted the number one lead generator in the real estate industry in Prescott, Arizona, later voted number one in the United States. Everything I did was entrepreneurial genius, and I loved creating and improving systems that made people money. After selling my real estate company due to health concerns related to mold exposure, I attempted retirement.

After a couple of years, however, boredom soon crept in, and I discovered another opportunity in the precious metals industry. As a successful precious metals dealer, I wanted to share my knowledge and help others achieve a six-figure income. Thus, I founded Scrap Gold University and partnered with aspiring entrepreneurs in this lucrative field, again drawing upon my experience.

Chapter 8

Nurturing Herb

It has become abundantly clear to me that God bestowed upon me a keen sense of intuition, particularly when it comes to marketing trends and analyzing past history to predict future outcomes. I have always been a people person, relishing in engaging conversations and learning from those around me. The power of observation has been one of my greatest gifts.

In 1980, my life took an unexpected turn. After my mother unceremoniously kicked my father out of our lives, I felt it was my time to step up and take care of him, to repay him for all he had done for me. Little did I know at the time that he was not my biological father. I have always suspected the 'secret' had much to do with the demise of their marriage. Oblivious to this revelation, I was driven by a desire to support and protect the man who had been there for me.

At that point, I had just completed three grueling years of strict probation for my second felony of selling marijuana to friends, falling victim to a setup. The judge wanted to send me to prison for three to five years, an unimaginable fate for a long-haired fair-complected hippie like me. By some stroke of divine grace, I managed to avoid that sentence. However, I continued down a reckless and fearless path, continuing to sell pot despite the looming threat of a third felony and a potential 20-year prison term. Street smarts became my shield. As a blue-eyed slender blonde boy with soft features, I was well aware of the danger of prison time, and the threat of so many years at such a young and impressionable age may have formed me into a lifelong hardened criminal. It is only by the grace of God that I was saved from such a destiny.

As my father found himself alone and unable to work due to a debilitating stroke, I felt it was time for us to leave Nebraska behind and start anew. We packed up my 1967 Dodge pickup and headed to Boulder, Colorado, where my lifelong best friend, Greg H., resided. By this point in my life, I had dabbled in numerous business ventures and side jobs, allowing me to avoid traditional employment and time clocks. Independence was my mantra.

Given our financial constraints, finding an affordable apartment seemed daunting. However, I scoured the newspaper ads for roommates, knowing that Boulder was a college town with numerous people seeking to rent their rooms. Would anyone be willing to accommodate a young hippie with a father in declining health? I was determined never to abandon him, unlike my mother. Thankfully, we stumbled upon a small basement apartment for $325 a month, conveniently located within walking distance of downtown Boulder, all utilities included.

As I sought ways to generate income, I recalled the roommate situation and decided to start a business called "Find a Roommate." For a fee of $35, I matched compatible individuals in need of housing. Surprisingly, the business thrived, opening doors for me to meet various male and female applicants. I was able to spend the summer basking in the lakes and hiking the mountain trails surrounding Boulder. I often had ulterior motives, hoping to use the opportunity to meet new people, particularly women. Despite my innate awkwardness and shyness, I managed to form many friendships because I had the capacity to be bold and brazen (or an eclectic mix of anything in between, it really depended on the company), spending my nights exploring the local bars in search of purpose and meaningful connections.

Simultaneously, my days were dedicated to caring for my father, who could no longer drive or manage daily tasks independently. I became his chauffeur, accompanying him to appointments and ensuring he had groceries. We spent countless hours together, knowing how lonely he felt, like a stranger in a foreign land, severed from everything he once held dear, including his beloved daughters, Lisa and Jodi.

During this tumultuous period, I encountered Jim, who owned a video dating service called "Two's Company." It didn't take long for us to realize that our businesses aligned seamlessly, and we decided to merge our efforts. Engrossed in the world of matchmaking, I reveled in examining the profiles of individuals searching for love. Witnessing their yearning for connection during the video business's nascent stage was heartwarming and gratifying. Our phone rang incessantly as we helped people pursue their love goals and find a place to call home—two of life's most significant pursuits.

Then came an offer I couldn't refuse—a cash offer that would grant me the luxury of ample free time while I searched for my next opportunity. I spent the summer basking in the lakes surrounding Boulder, accompanied by my lifelong friend Greg. We indulged in smoking pot, drinking beer, and relishing the carefree moments our generation often cherished.

While Greg toiled away at a factory job, I had no desire to follow suit.

As summer drew to a close, so did my nest egg. I reminisced about my time selling cars in Lincoln, Nebraska, back in 1977, working for a man named "Weird Wally" at Wally's Used Cars. Wally, AKA Rex S., was anything but ordinary; he was honest and valued truth above all else, even if it meant losing a sale. Under his guidance, I honed my sales skills while maintaining integrity and authenticity. He became my good friend and mentor.

Flipping through the Boulder newspaper, I discovered numerous job opportunities in car sales. Within hours, I landed a job at Boulevard Datsun, and within months, I rose to become their top salesperson, forming valuable friendships along the way. My life was shifting rapidly, transitioning from self-employment to working for someone else with set hours and a regular paycheck. Nevertheless, the satisfaction of making connections and positively impacting lives remained constant.

During this period, a friend of my father's, a young woman named Colette, visited Boulder. Colette had developed a close bond with my father back in Lincoln, and she confided in Greg, expressing her concern for his loneliness and longing for his daughters. Colette proposed taking him back to Lincoln, promising to care for him. Although devastated, I knew deep down that my father's happiness was paramount, even if it meant enduring further heartbreak. Thus, he left for Lincoln the following week. I frequently made the journey back to Lincoln, from Boulder, to visit my mother and sisters, so I could also keep a watchful eye on my father.

Chapter 9

Seeking Answers,
Finding Questions:
Losing Herb

When I first found out about the donor, I sank back into my chair, my brain numbed by the overwhelming shock and disbelief. Questions plagued my mind, wondering what kind of loving and noble God would allow such a cruel fate to befall a man as honorable and loving as my father. Later, it was revealed that he had spent over 14 years at the Beatrice State Home for Feeble-Minded Youth before being sterilized and released.

In the following months, I existed in a fog of mental confusion, surpassing even the haze I experienced during my drug use. I turned to God more than ever, desperately seeking His guidance to prevent my thoughts from spiraling into madness, or worse.

My visits to Nebraska from Colorado became more frequent as I tried to spend precious moments with my father. I no longer saw him through the same lens as before. A newfound appreciation blossomed within me for the man I had called Dad all those years. Memories flooded my mind—I imagined him saying, "That's my boy," countless times like he had every Saturday he wasn't working. Looking back, my father had known my entire life that I was not his genetic counterpart and had never behaved in any way other than a doting father would. That makes him beyond great in my book.

Sadly, the toll of decades spent working 60 to 70-hour weeks had taken its toll on his health. Six months after my startling revelation, my father, Herbert Wyatt, passed away on Thanksgiving Day, 1983. I had never let him know that I had discovered our genetic differences.

Despite a raging blizzard, people from all corners of the county made their way to Lincoln, Nebraska, to pay their respects to Shorty Wyatt. His friends and co-workers would respectfully pass his casket and pause to shake my hand, making sure to tell me what a great guy I had for a father. It was then that I realized how deeply loved, admired, and respected my father was. As his long-lost brothers, sisters, and cousins arrived, I couldn't shake the sense of disconnection and confusion, intensifying the bewilderment surrounding my own genetics. Most of his family knew about the 'situation' but would never tell me, remaining true to the lies and deception. Standing there that day, bidding my final farewells, I prayed to God for the strength to endure the difficult days ahead, even though I had no inkling of how challenging those future years would become.

In the following months, I tried to divert my attention from the pain of losing my father. My curiosity shifted towards the sperm donor, the man who had granted me life. I wondered what he looked like, where he lived, and what profession he pursued. Did he donate multiple times? Did he share my blonde hair? Most importantly, did he ever contemplate my existence?

Summoning my courage, I reached out to my mother's doctor—the same doctor who had delivered me 28 years earlier—hoping to uncover the missing pieces of my life. Nervously, I picked up the phone and, within minutes, found myself conversing with the man who held the answers. I explained the situation, how I had stumbled upon the secret, how much I cherished my father, and how he had recently passed away, leaving a void in my heart that only truth and understanding could fill.

"Do you remember the sperm donor, the man who gave me life?" I inquired.

To my dismay, the doctor couldn't recall anything specific. "Greg, we used quite a few donors back then," he replied. The revelation hit me hard—I had no idea how widespread the practice of sperm donation was in the 1950s.

Never one to give up, I showed up at his house to try again. In a hopeful gesture, he called for his wife to retrieve my mother's file from the basement. Over the years, he had delivered more than 19,000 babies, and I couldn't help but wonder how many of them were my biological siblings. Did I have a right to know?

Opening the musty and yellowed file, he smiled warmly and said, "Yes, I remember this well."

Silently, I whispered a prayer of gratitude to God. The initial urge to snatch the file from his hand and run out the door faded away, replaced by a calm acceptance.

"What kind of man was he?" I asked the doctor, eager to hear his description. A familiar chill ran down my spine as he began to paint a picture of the man who had contributed to my existence. The doctor's words formed a vivid image of a person who bore a striking resemblance to myself— a man who resembled me in every way: blonde hair, broad shoulders, smartly dressed, intelligent, witty, and pursuing a Ph.D. A chill ran down my spine. I was able to glance my mother's file as he looked it over and noted the WK. Curiosity got the best of me, and Dr. Thierstein let me know that they inverted the donor initials. I would savor this information away for another day and time.

Over the following months, the doctor and I grew closer, bonded by our shared understanding of my unique predicament, and I respected his need to maintain patient confidentiality. "The privacy of our patients is paramount," he emphasized. However, he acknowledged the legitimacy of my quest for answers. I could see his health deteriorating, and as his condition worsened, I realized my time with him was limited. Shortly before his passing, he entrusted me with the name of the man who fathered me. Within weeks, he departed, and my quest took a new direction. I carried that name in my wallet for days, which turned into weeks, months, and years, allowing my imagination to run wild. Not only that, I was scared.

I often pondered the whereabouts and circumstances of this man, but more importantly, I wondered if he would accept a son like me. My diligent search for information on artificial insemination proved fruitless. One night, I perused an encyclopedia at my mother's house, a resource I had once used for my high school studies, and looked up "artificial insemination." To my disappointment, it contained only a brief three-word reference: "See animal breeding."

I bought a twelve-pack of beer to bury my anxieties, smoked several joints, and attempted to push the matter aside again. For a while, it worked.

This escape mechanism worked for a time, momentarily easing my troubled mind. But deep down, I was haunted by my humanity, my sense of self. Was I some kind of scientific experiment, a creation akin to Frankenstein? From there, I discovered eugenics.

Chapter 10

Connecting the Dots:

The Search for Biological Siblings

After receiving my donor's name from the doctor, which I had carried in my wallet for what seemed like an eternity, I felt compelled to take the next step and revisit the doctor. To my surprise, I discovered he had passed away, leaving his wife alone. Then, I realized I had a new mission: to find my biological father and locate my lost siblings. Motivation for this task was exacerbated by my status as fatherless. While Herb was alive, I had abandoned searching past the donor's name, but now that he was gone I had to honor my curiosity. The conspiracy of silence was ringing loudly in my ears. Being an only child, I had always yearned for a brother with whom I could share a connection and genetic similarities that I thought were forever lost.

When I knocked on Mrs. Thierstein's door, she greeted me warmly. I thanked her for allowing me to discover my true identity and embrace my heritage. I explained that I intended to find the names of my half-siblings—the children of other mothers who had used the same donor. I assured her I had no intention of causing any trouble and had no plans to contact them except for a brother, if I should find one. It was a slight lie, as I knew deep down that I would eventually seek out and contact any siblings I found. The challenge was that they probably did not realize I existed. Despite the discomfort of the situation, I knew I had to push forward to find closure.

Mrs. Thierstein led me down to the basement, where the fragments of my past were meticulously organized like soldiers preparing for war. I couldn't believe my eyes as I beheld rows upon rows of meticulously arranged manila file folders, categorized by year. Questions of legality crossed my mind as I wondered whether what I was doing or what the doctor had done was lawful or ethical. However, at that moment, none of that mattered. This opportunity was bestowed upon me to piece together my shattered past after years of praying for the truth and yearning to discover my true identity.

Overwhelmed, I pulled up a chair and surveyed the tens of thousands of records, feeling my blood pressure rise. Starting at the top left-hand corner, I began meticulously searching through the folders, examining each one. I pulled out the first folder and carefully noted the name, familiarizing myself with Dr. Thierstein's system.

The first delivery listed in his private practice records was from September 1946. I delved into the folders for that month, searching for my mother's records, eager to uncover the details of the procedures that had taken place. Within minutes, I located the original documents that outlined my birth. Next to the word "insemination" were the inverted initials "KW." The donor's sperm had been injected into my mother on September 8th and September 9th, 1954. Dr. Thierstein had charged my mother $15 for each procedure.

It was challenging to process and comprehend how this revelation forever changed my future. As the day grew late, I decided to return early the next morning, unprepared for the emotional rollercoaster that awaited me.

I knew my donor had moved to my hometown in the early 1950s, but I had yet to learn when he had started donating to help childless couples conceive. Beginning there, I methodically searched through hundreds of records on the first day but came up empty-handed.

Driven by determination, I pressed on to find my lost siblings, regardless of the cost. Returning the following day, armed with my hot coffee, notebook, and pens, I created a makeshift desk to better organize myself for the daunting task ahead.

I decided to delve into my donor's wife's medical records and discovered they had welcomed a daughter in late 1954. They had become close friends with Dr. Thierstein, going out to dinner and attending social events together. I made sure to only remove my parents' file from the basement, never wanting to cause any trouble for anyone under any circumstances.

As time passed, Dr. Thierstein informed my biological father about his numerous patients struggling to conceive. He proposed donating his sperm to help childless couples, sharing the gift of life, to which Dr. Thierstein eagerly agreed, especially since it was a way to help struggling patients. My biological father saw this endeavor as only an opportunity to pay for university tuition. When Dr. Thierstein had asked why he was willing to make so many deposits, the donor casually answered that he knew his genes were superior and would help childless couples create superior children. His misguided ideas of eugenic perfection didn't take into account the mother's genes which means that the genetic soup of him and the birth mother could have created some very inferior issues—since humans mate by pheromones and many other factors. Furthermore, the way that the insemination was done, half-siblings could have eventually met and/or procreated since we were geographically in the same peer groups by age. There are more factors that need to be taken into account.

Returning to the files, I diligently numbered and organized my system, ensuring I would never lose the data that revealed my hidden past. I had no idea how many offspring I would find, and my mind raced, trying to fathom the potential number—could it be 10, 1000?

It was another beautiful spring morning in April 1989, and nearly six years had passed since I discovered the truth behind my secret conception. I thanked God my mother had revealed it to me when she did; I couldn't imagine a life without knowing the truth. In mere moments, I would embark on my third day in the basement, immersed in rows of files. I found myself again standing at the doctor's home, ready to continue my journey entwined with fate.

The doctor's wife knocked on the door and asked, "Greg, would you like some lunch." She was always so kind and considerate. Of course, I was obliged. After lunch, I resumed my search—a search that seemed to define my entire existence.

Returning to the files, it didn't take long before I stumbled upon my second sister's folder. Her name was Susan, and she was born on January 31st, 1955.

72

Then, to my delight, I made another discovery that day—Christi, born on June 18th, 1955.

Deciding to end the day early, I headed home to check on my mother and see how she was doing. I would always share the names and details of my findings with her. It struck me as intriguing that Christi was born just ten days after me, and a closer examination of the files revealed that we were conceived almost simultaneously. The donor had been quite busy.

When I mentioned Christi's last name, my mom turned pale. She revealed that Christi's family had been our next-door neighbors when I was born. She even had pictures of Christi and me playing together in our living room. Being the sentimental person she was, she retrieved a photo album containing several images. She recalled that Christi's father had also been at the Beatrice State Home for Feeble-Minded Youth and was likely sterilized like my father. This new information was difficult to process, and I questioned what was happening worldwide. While relieved to uncover these details, it also stirred up the demons that had plagued my mind. I managed to keep them at bay most days, but today wasn't one of them.

I kissed my mother on the cheek and headed to the liquor store, where I bought a six-pack of beer and rolled a couple of joints. Seeking solace, I went to the local neighborhood park, a place I had cherished since my youth. It was 3:00 in the afternoon, and the sun's warmth felt comforting. I lit up a joint, opened a beer, and tried to calm my racing thoughts as I contemplated the meaning behind all these revelations. Later, I would look up to the sky and ponder my existence in this world. *Does it ever get easier?* It's a good thing that question went unanswered, because the answer has been a steady no. It doesn't get easier, but it is worth it.

The following day, I returned to the doctor's home, feeling rejuvenated and focused on finding the brother I 'knew' was out there. Did he know about me? Was he searching for me? Did he resemble me or share similar struggles? These haunting questions had consumed me for far too long.

The third half-sister I discovered was named Diana, born on January 9th, 1955. Her name struck a familiarity chord, and I wondered where I knew her from. Suddenly, it hit me—we had attended high school together, and she had sat in front of me in biology class. We graduated in the same year, 1973, and I recalled being oddly drawn to her looks and personality. Fortunately, she wanted nothing to do with me; who knows what could have transpired otherwise?

My fourth half-sister, Susan, was born on January 30th, 1955. At the time, I jotted down her information without knowing who she was. However, I would later discover that her story was one of tragedy.

Lastly, my fifth sister, Cyndi, was born on August 25th, 1954.

A MOTHER'S LOVE

I want to take a moment to acknowledge my mother's unwavering support throughout this journey. She wholeheartedly embraced my search and encouraged me at every step, for which I could never thank her enough. Although I never explicitly expressed it, she knew how much it meant to me. Every day, from the moment I obtained my donor's name, I would share the details of my progress with her. I could see in her eyes that she was proud, knowing the person I had become, that no one could convince me otherwise when I set my mind to something—I would always prove them wrong.

Chapter 11

Dr. Thierstein's Influence

Dr. Thierstein, a name that holds immense significance in this story, emerges as one of the central heroes. He was the essence of an honest and ethical obstetrician. A headline in his obituary caught my attention read, "God was my partner," and in those few words, the essence of his character was beautifully summarized.

As I recall the setting of Dr. Thierstein's house, I feel compelled to search for his address, relying solely on my memory. Built in an era when the surrounding land was untouched countryside, the house stood proudly amidst gentle rolling hills, adorned with vibrant green grass and framed by an unblemished blue sky.

The Thierstein family, the original inhabitants of the house, held a profound love for horses. Their sprawling property outside of Lincoln, constructed in the 1956, boasted stables that housed their own equestrian companions. It was a raised ranch, with a garage underneath and ample storage space. Every inch of the property was thoroughly maintained, mirroring the meticulousness of a doctor's nature. Upon stepping inside, one would be greeted by plaques and photographs, testaments to Dr. Thierstein's achievements.

I recall a conversation during which he revealed that he had actually adopted a client's baby, rescuing the child from an abortion. The mother was a poor young single woman who lived life in poverty and was looking for help and guidance. Both single motherhood and abortion were pretty much out of the question in those days. Her baby became Dr. Thierstein and his wife's daughter.

Dr. Thierstein's wife, his trusted assistant, shared an inseparable bond with him. They complemented each other perfectly, radiating happiness, perpetually adorned with smiles. His doctor's office mirrored this aura of joy, instilling a sense of comfort and reassurance in all who entered.

He personified the archetypal doctor of yesteryears, and indeed, what doctors should strive to be today. Untouched by corruption, he possessed a heart of pure gold. His guiding mantra was rooted in placing God first, others second, and himself last. Back in those days, the issues plaguing our modern food landscape had yet to surface, and both Dr. Thierstein and his wife maintained slender and healthy figures. Neither of them were particularly tall or robust, and their overall appearance testified to their commitment to holistic well-being.

From my earliest recollections, I can vividly remember my mother taking me to see Dr. Thierstein for both her own health concerns and mine. There was always a genuine fondness in his demeanor towards me. I recall him affectionately patting me on the head, remarking, "Well, you've turned out to be a real fine young lad."

Every few years, we would visit his office, and each time, he exhibited a genuine interest in my well-being. His warmth and friendliness never waned. However, as I grew older, our encounters became less frequent, until that fateful meeting at his house, many years later. At that time, I had no inkling of what lay ahead.

Chapter 12

Journey to Blacksburg:

Seeking Pieces of Identity

Let's look at the facts quickly before going into details. I lived in Denver, Colorado, from 1980 to 1995. It took me 8 years, one month, and one day from the time I found out on June 8th, 1983, until I shook the donor, Kroontje's, hand on July 9th, 1991.

The drive from Pensacola, Florida, to Blacksburg, Virginia, was 739 miles, approximately 11 hours in a car with a failing clutch. Had I endeavored to make the trip from Denver, Colorado to Blacksburg, it would have been 1,490 miles and 22 hours non-stop. I prayed that my car would make it back to my condo, relying on the grace of God. When I pulled up to my condo, after this trip, I had less than $20 in my pocket and my clutch went out completely. To top it off, my rent was due the next week. I had never been in that financial position situation before, but it was a small price to pay for the satisfaction I received. I was afraid if I didn't go at this point, I wouldn't have made the trip at all. I'm glad I followed that instinct. Now, let me share the story in more vivid detail.

I had achieved considerable success running door-to-door marketing programs with my sales crew for various businesses over the years. Recently, I had secured an account with a company in Pensacola, Florida. After weeks of preparation, including assembling promotional items and signing contracts, I was ready to implement my business program.

However, I needed to account for the weather, which had escaped me for the first season of business. The rainy season had engulfed Pensacola, and the stifling temperatures and 100% humidity made every task a challenge.

As I ventured into the neighborhoods to assess the market, I quickly realized that the people of Pensacola were vastly different from those in the Midwest. It became apparent that I would face an uphill battle, a rare occurrence that brought discouragement to my determined spirit.

Sitting in my motel room one evening, I decided to return home the next day. Giving up or accepting failure was not typical of me, but the circumstances seemed insurmountable. At this point, I was left with a mere $700 to my name. Amid my contemplation, a thought struck me: *How far was Blacksburg, Virginia, from Pensacola, Florida?*

Back then, I turned to a map for answers, in the absence of computers. It appeared relatively close, though gauging distances accurately on a small map proved challenging. Little did I know, the journey would encompass 739 miles, an 11-hour and 9-minute drive, one way. From the map, it had appeared to be a mere 400-mile trip, the balance of the extension of the trip was consumed by the increasing familiar twinge of stress and nerves in the pit of my stomach.

Considering I might never be this close to Blacksburg again, I resolved to embark on the trip, not to meet my biological father but to explore where he had spent several decades teaching at the University of Virginia Tech. This journey could uncover a wealth of information, filling the void within me and, perhaps, offering closure.

The refusal to give me what little I asked for, information and a meeting, seemed at odds with his character. He had been 'Citizen of the Year,' 'Teacher of the Year,' among many other accolades. When he had first arrived in Blacksburg, it was a mostly all-male school, entrenched in tradition and old-school ways. My donor father advocated for women until VT admitted them. He also got his hands on the banned books list, books he had read during his early days in America, and made them available outside of his classroom, encouraging students to read them, despite the hot water it got him into. While the pain of his rejection boiled inside of me, my curiosity stemmed from how alike we were having never interacted. He was not a part of my life in any way, shape, or form, other than his initial contribution, and yet we were both happy and able to poke proverbial bears when the bears needed a good poking.

My 1978 Datsun B210 car was fuel-efficient but plagued with issues. The air conditioning had long ceased functioning, subjecting me to constant sweat and discomfort. Moreover, the clutch gradually deteriorated, and I could feel its weakening grip. Anxiety consumed me throughout the trip as I wondered if my car would survive the journey back. Financially, I had never been so destitute. At 36 years old, these circumstances tested my resolve.

The state's breathtaking beauty unfolded as I drove into Virginia and neared Blacksburg. I marveled that my biological father had chosen such a picturesque place to call home, a place that looked like Boulder. I found lodging at a local motel just outside the city. Its vintage appearance harkened back to the 1950s. I couldn't help but wonder if my biological father had once stayed there after his long journey from Lincoln Commons, Nebraska more than thirty years ago. The elaborate beauty of the Smoky Mountains was able to capture my awe, never failing to remind me of our smallness in such a large and incredible world.

The following day, armed with notebooks and pens, I went to the University of Virginia Tech. Since it was summertime, the campus was relatively quiet, with only a few summer school students dotting the landscape. This serendipitous circumstance made my exploration easier, although a tinge of stress lingered.

As I traversed the campus, I envisioned the life my biological father had led there. Imagining him teaching thousands of students and preparing them for their careers, I couldn't help but wonder why he had shown no care for me. Was he hiding something? My mind became a whirlwind of unanswerable questions and unimaginable truths.

Over the next couple of days, I painstakingly gathered every shred of information I could find, and there was an abundance of it. My donor had enjoyed great success and garnered immense respect throughout his career.

My final stop was at the administration building, home to meticulously organized archives of students and teachers. Among the troves of documents, I stumbled upon a photograph of him, captured on his 65th birthday. It was labeled as his retirement picture, though he had never retired. Instead, he had moved on to even more prosperous endeavors, spearheading the development of Warm Hearth Village, one of the largest retirement communities at that time. He took great pride in that accomplishment, a project spanning two decades to fruition.

Filled with the weight of newfound knowledge, I packed my belongings on that fateful day and embarked on my journey. I glanced in the rearview mirror as I departed from the city, knowing this opportunity would never reoccur. It was my only chance to extend my gratitude by shaking my donor's hand and thanking him for the gift of life. My desire for a relationship had never been my intention; all I sought was information—a theme that had permeated this journey in my life.

I abruptly turned the car around, consulting one of my books for his address, which I had carefully recorded. Within moments, I arrived at Warm Hearth Village and parked in front of his house. My heart raced within my chest, and nerves wracked my body. Part of me wanted to flee, but I knew I would never forgive myself if I did.

Awkwardly, I approached the door and rang the doorbell. An older gentleman, tall and muscular, answered, peering at me over his glasses with a perplexed expression. "Yes, can I help you?" he inquired.

My mind raced, grappling with the question of how to proceed. I simply blurted out, "I'm Greg Wyatt."

He seemed to mistake me for one of his former students. "Greg Wyatt? Where do I know you from?

How do I know you?" he asked, his face confused and curious.

Reaching out, I extended my hand and repeated, "I'm Greg Wyatt. I just wanted to thank you for giving me the gift of life. I want to assure you that I don't want any money, and I'll never bother you again." With those words hanging in the air, I abruptly turned and walked away, never to lay eyes on him again.

By the time I opened my car door after retreating, his world was swirling around him. It might be cooler to say that I didn't look at him again, but as I glimpsed, it was clear that the realization of who I was to him was washing over him, hitting him like a ton of bricks. The same reaction was boiling inside me, this man gave so little thought to who I was or what I was doing that he couldn't drag my name through the vast wheel wells of his mind until I had stated who I was in entirety. I was, in effect, nobody to him, yet my quest to find out all I could about him had at times overwhelmed me.

Chapter 13

Reunion and Rejection: Christi

My sister Christi O. came into this world just ten days after me in 1955. Discovering her existence was significant, and I couldn't wait to share the news with my mother.

I rushed home excitedly, ready to update my mom on another sibling. She always showed enthusiasm and interest whenever I discussed my search, which became a bonding experience, even if I didn't realize it at the time. As I handed her the card, I couldn't contain my anticipation.

"Mom, I found another one! Her name is Christi," I exclaimed.

Her eyes widened with surprise. "Oh, Greg, I can't believe it! The Os were our next-door neighbors when you kids were born. I even have a picture of you playing together in the photo album. Let me find it." She hurriedly retrieved the album, and my mind raced with possibilities. What if we had dated, married, and started a family without knowing the truth? It was one of the many reasons I had embarked on this search— to prevent such complications.

As my mother returned with the album, excitement and apprehension consumed me. I carefully turned the pages, and there it was—a photograph capturing the two of us playing together on the floor at seven months old.

"Look, Mom! It's us," I said, my voice trembling. The realization sent chills down my spine, and my head spun. It was an overwhelming moment filled with both joy and uncertainty.

She gazed at the picture, nostalgia evident in her eyes. "Wayne and Rowena were your dad's and my friends, personally. We used to have them over for dinner and spend time together. You and Christi would play together," she recalled.

Then, a bombshell dropped. My mother's face turned grave as she revealed, "I remember them mentioning once that Wayne was also in Beatrice State Home, just like your dad. They even went to the same doctor and underwent successful insemination with the same donor. It's incredible how our lives intertwined without anyone knowing. It makes me glad we discovered the truth."

Hearing this information both pleased and unsettled me. Sharing the same donor with Christi's family made me feel sick, but it also brought a sense of completeness to my search.

Living in Denver since 1980, I often traveled back to Lincoln, which allowed me to delve deep into my research. In those pre-internet days, I relied heavily on city directories and old phone books at the library, painstakingly piecing together the puzzle. The logical first step was starting with our parents' names, knowing that the women's maiden names would have changed after marriage.

I discovered Christi's number and address in a city directory within a few months. Like me, her husband, Ken H., had also attended Lincoln Northeast High School. I mustered the courage to drive by her address and caught a glimpse of three young children playing in the front yard. They were my nieces and nephews, unbeknownst to them, and I doubted they would ever find out or even care. It left me grappling with complex questions about the nature of family and the significance of blood ties as I noted that her children were just like her and me with the blonde, fair complexion playing with not a care in the world. Confusion clouded my thoughts as I made regular drives past that house, afraid to reach out and disrupt their lives, much like mine had been disrupted.

Eventually, in 1993, I found the strength to call Christi and disclose my belief that I was her long-lost brother. However, she initially dismissed me as a quack, questioning my authenticity. "How do I know you're real?" she asked skeptically.

Taking a chance, I responded, "You can call Dr. Thierstein, your mom's pediatrician. Although he's no longer alive, his wife knows about my search."

A sudden realization hit me, causing a wave of panic. I had inadvertently betrayed the kind-hearted people who had assisted me in uncovering my identity. There were no words to express the pain of my confusion. I anxiously awaited Christi's call, unsure what to say to salvage the situation, contemplating my own selfishness.

Shortly afterward, the phone rang. Dr. Thierstein's wife was clearly upset about my contact with Christi. She confronted me in a state of distress, leaving me at a loss for words. Regret filled my heart as I contemplated the consequences of my actions. How could I have jeopardized the trust and privacy of those who had helped me? There were no words to express the magnitude of my pain.

Despite the turmoil, Christi and I decided to meet. Our reunion was nothing short of magical. The similarities in our physical appearance were astonishing, a testament to the strong genes of the donor that resonated through each of us and our other siblings. Christi rejected a relationship with me under the premise that her husband thought our relationship was strange, and it was for her too since while we were blood related, by design we belonged to different family structures and were never meant to have met or even known about each other. After she withdrew from having a relationship with me, I moved onto the next name on my list.

Years later, on April 30th, 1989, I sat down to fill out a card, meticulously documenting my research. This card held the key to my journey, waiting to be unlocked someday. Although my memory had started to fade, I could still recall the precise order of our meetings and other significant events, except for a few dates. Writing the information, names, my findings down preserved the information so I could accurately represent my journey, when the day, such as this would come, for me to write a more substantial work.

Chapter 14

The Search Continues: Cyndi

The file shows the number 141, but that has to be an error. Interestingly, numbers identify human beings over their real persona. It reminds me of the Holocaust, only backwards because the numbers, in my case, matched anonymous faces, nothing more, nothing less. I had their names, but they were unknowns to me—the depersonalization of humanity changes forms, not intent.

My first discovery came on April 27th, 1989, when I found Cyndi's file. It was the first one, making me wonder how many others were there. I was searching for that elusive brother; a record I knew I would never find but one that fueled my determination to keep going through this madness.

This was just the beginning of my investigation. At this point, these individuals were just ink on paper, lacking real personalities. So, I took each card and carefully jotted down my notes for further investigation.

Cyndi, Christi, Diana, Susan, and Susie. Five biological, blood-related half-siblings, but no brother. Adding myself to the equation, six individuals were conceived from this donor's egg, his contribution to society. My investigation took on a new direction, one that would span decades.

Cyndi was the first offspring I discovered; ironically enough, she would be the only one with whom a meaningful relationship would develop. But as time passed, our lives diverged, heading in separate directions. It was important to remember that the genetic component linking us held no social meaning, as our lives lacked shared memories to build upon. It was a tragic realization, an emotion I had not considered initially. Were these sisters my family? Did we have a foundation of shared experiences, or were our paths empty and hollow regarding our relationships?

So, in earnest, I began seeking information at local public libraries in Lincoln, Nebraska. I sifted through old telephone books and city directories, trying to cross-reference and find the information I wasn't even sure I deserved to have. It created a conflict within my mind, but I pressed on regardless. I was determined not to fail, especially after coming this far.

I found Cyndi's address, her parents' address from the '70s, and looked it up. It was only about 29 miles from my mother's house in Ashland, Nebraska. Her parents had lived there for many years, shedding light on the high school she attended—Waverly High School. That led me to the yearbook, where she graduated in 1972. The picture in the yearbook was hauntingly familiar—it mirrored me. Her smile, her hair—everything about her image resonated with me. I carefully noted down her phone number and her mother's number. I also became aware that her current name would not be the same as back then, making it even more challenging, especially after she married. These pages of information remained in my possession for years before I mustered up enough courage to take the next step.

However, on July 2nd, 1989, I finally gathered the strength to make a call. According to my notes, this was the conversation:

"Hello, Mrs. E., my name is Greg Wyatt, and I went to high school with your daughter Cyndi." It was a little white lie, but it allowed me to continue, stumbling through the following sentence, "A nice jovial lady," as my notes described her.

"I don't want to upset you, Mrs. E., but I was wondering if you've ever told Cyndi how special she was, that our families have something in common," I said. The words spilled out, and momentarily, I questioned whether I was causing harm in pursuing my search. Guilt and sickness washed over me. *Should I even be doing what I'm doing?*

She told me I was mistaken, that there was no way. At that moment, I thought I was just messing up other people's lives at the expense of my search. It was a conflicting experience that left me feeling guilty and uncertain.

Years would pass before I mustered up the courage to delve back into that card and continue my investigation. Her denial plunged me back into the conspiracy of silence, except now I was perpetrating the silence on myself. There was no one to blame, the shroud draped over the secretive past was permeating my soul, making my outlook bleak. If no one would speak openly and if many donor offspring didn't even know about their origin, how was I to make a difference?

Every few months, when visiting my mother in Lincoln, Nebraska, I would pull out my cards and dive deeper into my investigations, despite a part of me urging me to stop. I was tired of facing rejection and hitting dead ends in a situation that seemed never-ending.

On March 31st, 1993, almost four years after finding Cyndi's name in the file, I intensified my investigation into her past. I was clearly obsessed, desperately seeking a friendly voice and a reassuring smile that would tell me everything was okay.

To my surprise, Cyndi reacted positively when I shared the details of my journey. She was upbeat and supportive, which caught me off guard. I told her I had reason to believe she was my half-sister, recounting how I came across the information. Now, I faced the challenge of proving the truth of my claims, but back then, DNA tests were not an option, leaving me backed into a corner again.

Knowing that Dr. Thierstein had passed away, but his wife was still living alone in that house, I broke my cardinal rule and suggested to Cyndi that she should call his wife.

Within a week, she called me back, and in her jovial manner, she confirmed, "I guess you are right. I am your half-sister." All the struggles and years of searching felt worthwhile for a fleeting moment.

Meeting Cyndi became a goal of mine, and I suggested it in 1995, after having married Joyce. I was back in Lincoln, and we were able to meet.

Cyndi worked for a major insurance company that specialized in working with hospitals and doctors. When she arrived at the door, I greeted her with a handshake and a hug. It was the first time I had ever physically touched someone genetically related to me in this situation in my life. Cyndi handled it gracefully, with intelligent eloquence.

We exchanged pleasantries and phone numbers, and we shared stories about our lives over the next several months. When I told her about approaching her mom, she informed me that her mother had passed away several years prior, and she hoped that my revelation hadn't caused her premature death. She mentioned it nonchalantly, sharing that her father had passed away ten years before, and she and her mother were very close.

It had taken me over ten long years to get this far, but I remained determined. I still had three other siblings to find.

Chapter 15

Navigating the Complexity of Reproductive Science:

My Philosophy on Donor Conception

In my opinion, reproductive science is an extension of eugenics. More recently, mankind has pivoted from trying to control reproduction to making having a family more readily available to those that have difficulties, turning something evil into something good, as intended by God. Here, I do not speak of abortion, which is negative eugenics, although is often improperly labeled.

Reflecting back to the '80s, it took me years to reconnect with my lost family, and the experience was bittersweet. Fast forward to today, and the landscape has changed significantly. Instead of reproductive science being treated like a dirty little secret that no one should discuss, people are very open about the help they receive in starting families. This transition makes writing this book much easier than it would have been several decades ago, and I like to think the crusaders of my generation had something to do with that. It may be too late for us to salvage our families and our past, but the goal was always to improve the future.

Sperm donation is now openly discussed, accepted, and utilized in many situations that were once considered taboo. While I may not feel comfortable with specific scenarios, such as two moms raising a child, I understand that love can conquer all, regardless of the complexity of relationships.

Presently, the offspring of sperm donors are not shrouded in secrecy as they were in the past, which is a positive development. Honesty and openness should always be encouraged. Society has often leaned towards fear-based living. Mankind often swaps out their poison being imbibed. The artificial insemination of the past took away the ability to ask origin questions, which are the most basic of all questions: Who am I? Why and how am I here? We need only look back in time at the Darwinian task of explaining our origins. What is most relevant? What protozoa or species of monkey they think we came from—or our current genetic makeup, while we are alive? Back then, it was overlooked that a person created from a highly gifted donor would naturally be curious about their origins and want to know more about their heritage.

Today, a sperm donor offspring can simply go online and find hundreds of potential half-siblings on platforms like Facebook or any variety of DNA testing site. They can even come across family reunions with 10 or 20, sometimes hundreds of children, all born from the same donor, some within days and months of each other. While I was not afforded such opportunities, connecting with others who share a similar background is a positive thing that I feel needs to be available. The generation of donor offspring that I belong to often felt disconnected due to our unique circumstances. Our parents were embarrassed by their genetic shortcomings and inability to create life without help since that was the supreme goal—

procreation. A stay-at-home wife was no doting postcard mother if she didn't produce offspring.

I remember being part of the Donor Offspring movement in the '80s when only a small number of us, perhaps two or three, were aware of our unconventional conceptions. We all shared similar feelings and experiences, and connecting with others who understood was comforting. As activists, our goal was to advocate for the rights of donor-conceived individuals and push for changes in laws to eliminate anonymity. We would spend hours upon hours on the phone strategizing our approach to meet these end results.

Interestingly, a few months ago, I discovered that anonymous sperm donation has become more regulated due to our activism. I stumbled upon a letter in my files confirming that our efforts had made an impact, which was a pleasant surprise. It is always nice to see the fruit of your efforts rewarded, even if its decades later. I have never attempted to bring awareness to any worthy cause without throwing my entire being into the work. In later books, we will be discussing other areas of my activism.

Reproductive science has grown to encompass donor eggs, frozen embryos, IVF, and the destruction of embryos. I participated in early scientific experiments, which eventually evolved into a medical industry that monetized both miseries and provided solace. It's a case of creating a need and offering a solution, a strategy I learned in business—creating a need ensures success in most cases.

Donor eggs seem acceptable, and the use of sperm donors is also widely acknowledged. However, freezing embryos, selectively choosing embryos, and destroying embryos can be seen as man playing God and pushing the boundaries of medicine. It's an industry that has blurred ethical lines. This will get messier as they genetically select certain traits to "turn-off" and "turn on," which is a socially acceptable way of saying that science will be able to fully engineer and artificially select genetics. The end goal still seems science fiction, but with more public talk of artificial wombs and designer babies, it may be more believable to the crowd that has stayed silent and disconnected from this issue for so long.

Many long-term studies have been initiated, but it remains to be seen if they will ever come to fruition. As with many things, people tend to focus on the present without considering the long-term consequences. It's the nature of our world. When demand is high and profits are assured, caution gets thrown to the wind. The macabre reality is they are playing with the soul of humanity—will an artificial womb (in the future, we are looking ahead) afford the same connection and ability to comfort and nurture that natural pregnancy creates?

We see loving homes that adopt and use reproductive services create success stories, but if you stick around you'll see the ugly dark side of the industry. That was the motivation for telling my story. I had loving parents who chose and wanted me, but something inside me would reach out, a thorn in my flesh, nagging that something wasn't quite right. As much as I attempted to push that anxiety aside, it turned out that it wasn't misplaced growing pangs. That festering knowledge was the truth of my conception, that though perpetuated before my mind's memory bank began, my body had stored the genetic anomaly and refused to let go until I had the truth.

In the '80s, I discovered Annette Barron and Ruben Pannor who wrote the book titled *The Shocking Consequences of Donor Insemination*. When I first heard of the project, they were looking for donor offspring to take part in the research that formed the book. My participation leant credibility to my plight and cause as the child of a donor and helped build what I was doing for other people like me. Annette and Ruben were good people. Both of these kind souls are now deceased. This book helped alleviate my disconnect and provided a sense of identity. It was a relief to realize I was not alone in my experiences. At that time, I felt incredibly isolated, and connecting with other donor offspring was immensely valuable, even if it was just a handful of people that could relate to my plight.

I would also like to note and credit the late Candice Turner, who was the original founder of Donor's offspring. Also, of great significance and note is Bill Cordray, who was my best friend and mentor through this process. He was one of the original pioneers in our pivotal movement. Both were also donor offspring, and while we didn't share donors, they were the first I connected with out of the handful of donor offspring that knew the truth of their origins. I am still grateful for our commonalities and strong bond.

The memories from that period remain etched deeply in my soul and mind. While the experience hasn't always positively impacted my well-being and longevity, I consider myself a survivor. Moreover, I've become aware that many others face even more challenging situations, which creates a sense of gratitude that rises up in me alongside the fighting spirit to make sure our voices and struggles aren't silenced by the cold indifference of the scientific and medical communities in the name of advancement.

Chapter 16

Reflecting on the Advancements in Reproductive Science

Looking back on the advancements in reproductive science, particularly after learning the truth in 1983, I couldn't help but contemplate the multitude of developments in reproductive rights, cloning, egg and sperm donation, in vitro fertilization (IVF), embryo freezing, and the ethical questions surrounding embryo selection and destruction.

As someone who personally experienced the complexities of these procedures, I hold a unique perspective on the matter. However, when discussing it publicly, I faced skepticism and gaslighting. People dismissively say, "If they hadn't done it, you wouldn't be here."

My stance strongly favors the abolition of anonymous sperm donation, deeming it necessary to make it illegal. The concept of creating anonymous individuals through anonymous donors strikes me as unfathomable. Every person deserves to know their heritage, genetic makeup, and background, especially regarding traits associated with intelligence and notions of superiority based on eugenics.

I can't comprehend how society can be so short-sighted as to believe that individuals conceived with highly gifted donors would not naturally be curious to know their origins. The act of lying about one's conception felt criminal to me. It was disheartening to realize that over a million donor-conceived individuals existed, with only a handful aware of the truth behind their conception. Nowadays, the internet has changed the landscape, allowing easier access to information, which I find somewhat frustrating as I had to undergo a tumultuous journey with limited results. Yet, discovering my true identity was priceless. However, the absence of relationships and connections left a profound emotional and mental toll, and I harbored deep resentment toward the system.

It was evident that financial motivations played a significant role in these practices, emphasizing the prominence of money above all else.

Chapter 17

My Mother's Last Wish:
Moments of Love and Closure

If it weren't for the tragic loss of my mother, I wouldn't be here today, sharing this story with you. Her lifelong habit of smoking had taken a toll on her health, and in 1993, she visited the doctor who warned her that if she continued smoking, her days were numbered. With her lung function declining to a mere 20%, I accompanied her to that fateful appointment, waiting anxiously in the reception area.

Out of nowhere, a piercing scream shattered the calm of the waiting room. It sent chills down my spine, akin to the sound of a helpless cat being struck by a passing car. Thirty agonizing minutes later, my mother emerged from the doctor's office and entered the receptionist's room. I couldn't contain my curiosity and blurted out, "Mom, who was that screaming like that?" To my surprise, behind teary eyes, she replied, "That was me." The medical staff had struggled to find a vein to measure her plummeting oxygen levels in the bloodstream.

Overwhelmed by the situation, my mother made her way to the car, and I mustered the courage to approach the doctor, seeking answers in those fleeting 10 seconds. Having attended countless appointments with my mother, I needed to know how long she could endure such suffering. The doctor compassionately explained, "I see cases like these daily, and rarely do my patients last over a year. It's a heartbreaking reality."

At that very moment, a life-altering decision took hold of me. I knew I had to leave Denver, Colorado, and return to my hometown in Lincoln, Nebraska, to provide my mother with any support I could offer. Determined to take action, I sold my horse property in Fairplay, Colorado, and with the proceeds, purchased a modest yet rundown house in Weston, Nebraska, paying in cash. It was a time when frugality became my way of life, surviving on a meager $567 per month. Yes, that's right—every payment, expense, and necessity was meticulously tracked. I lived debt-free, owning my house outright, with no outstanding loans or financial obligations. My two twenty-year-old cars were also paid off. It was a life shaped by strict budgeting, where every penny had a purpose. Remarkably, I made $567 a month cover all my needs.

Another poignant detail is that my mother had attempted to quit smoking ten years before but hadn't fully stopped. The damage had already been done. People often fail to realize the impending danger of smoking, blindly marching towards a bleak fate. Although she had strived to quit, it was too late to undo the harm. I want to acknowledge that she successfully abstained from smoking during her pregnancy with me and continued for a few years after that.

Her last couple of years were devastating. I witnessed her transition from a vibrant and healthy woman to a frail, osteoporosis-ridden figure, just a mere shadow of her former self. She would endure relentless fits of coughing, up to 500 times per hour, struggling to catch her breath. Eventually, she found

106

herself in a nursing home where I frequently spent precious moments with her. During one of our final visits, she pleaded with me to bring her back to her cherished home in Havelock, along with her loyal companion, Tiffany, their beloved dog. How could I deny her plea or turn a blind eye to her request?

Taking on the role of her primary caregiver, we reconfigured the house to accommodate her wheelchair, even installing a hospital bed to ensure her comfort. On those initial nights, I stayed by her side, attentive to her needs. In the darkness, she would call my name, "Greg, Greg, are you there?" She became more childlike. I could see the little girl buried deep within her soul as she got closer to death. It became a full-time responsibility, and after a couple of days of witnessing her immense suffering, I realized that she required extensive care beyond what I could provide. There is something so painful when a son loses his mother, the woman who gave him life. To that point in my life, losing my mother had been the hardest thing for me to endure.

Chapter 18

Seeking Closure:
The Dearth of Silence

Five long years passed, filled with desperation and longing. I could no longer bear the weight of uncertainty. Finally, summoning all my courage, I confronted my demons head-on and sought closure. I embarked on an investigative journey, determined to locate my biological father once and for all. Yet, uncertainty lingered—what would happen next?

Through my decades-long standing with the local church, I confided in my pastor and enlisted his help as an intermediary. He acted on my behalf and made the initial call to the donor. When confronted with the truth, he neither confirmed nor denied it, requesting time for contemplation. A week later, on February 11th, 1988, he returned the call, leaving a message on my pastor's answering machine. His words conveyed disinterest in meeting me but reassured me that I came from "good genetic stock," ending the call with a request for no further contact. It was yet another distressing event in a seemingly endless series of misfortunes.

Yet, there remained a glimmer of hope, as my pastor explained that such initial responses were not uncommon in cases involving adoptees and birth parents. His words briefly reignited a flicker of hope within me. So, with the anticipation of a positive outcome or a change of heart, I chose to temporarily set the matter aside. Months passed, yet nothing changed.

When I wrote this letter, seven years had elapsed, and despite the distance I had traveled, the day I unraveled my secret felt perpetual. I longed for healing, closure, and the ability to move forward. So, I composed a letter to him, pouring out my emotions and articulating my desires with utmost clarity, laying it all bare. Here is a copy of what I wrote:

Dear Sir,

As time passes, it becomes clear that we may never have the opportunity to chat or speak man-to-man, to communicate as two people whose lives have intertwined remarkably. Over the last seven years, my life has significantly changed since that moment on July 9th, 1991. I hope that out of human decency, you will take the time to read the account of my life, which is intertwined with yours. I possess numerous talents and gifts that remained shrouded in mystery for the first 30 years of my existence. I was an enigma to myself. I always hoped that our encounter would turn the tide of fate. However, today the tides of my life crash relentlessly on the shores of time, sinking even deeper into the sands of curiosity.

I do not request a meeting, though nothing would bring me greater joy. I merely ask that you become an audience member in the play that you played a part in producing, a play that God scripted exclusively for me.

Thankfully, I have a wonderful wife, but otherwise, I am an orphan since my mother's passing on September 17th, 1995, and my father's on Thanksgiving Day in 1983. I was their only child until I turned 10. I had no biological siblings, but then my parents adopted two orphans from Korea in 1965. My mother was indeed a pioneer, and my love for them knows no bounds. My father, however, was unable to conceive as he

110

had been sterilized at the Beatrice State Home in Nebraska in 1945. In the eyes of eugenics, he was deemed defective. These people sought to create a stronger, purer race in America. Even in 1939, Time magazine named Hitler its Man of the Year.

During that era, being impoverished in America was, in some cases, treated as a crime. But had all these events not unfolded, I would not be writing this letter to you. I struggled to come to terms with this reality for many years, and I believe you can understand my turmoil.

In 1983, my father passed away as a broken man at the age of 59, having suffered a series of strokes that left him incapacitated and childlike in his demeanor. Just months before his illness, my mother divulged the details of my father's sterilization and my conception by Dr. Thierstein. She had been explicitly instructed never to share this information with me or anyone else. She genuinely believed that she had committed a crime. Perhaps you can comprehend why I previously worried about my health, as I had strived so hard to emulate my father and had failed so miserably. Discovering this truth freed me from the bondage of lies and left me confused and curious.

I prayed fervently to God to guide me to the man who granted me life, even though I was told it was an impossible endeavor. Yet, I continued to pray with even greater determination. God has worked wonders in my life, bringing me this far. I could not ask for more except for you to understand who I am and for me to learn who you are.

I can now understand, in a different way, why you were initially reluctant and then insistent on not meeting. When I traveled to Blacksburg in 1991, it was not to meet you per se but rather to discover more about myself by delving into your life. For a week, I followed the trail of your footsteps over the past 18 years. I must admit, I was pleased but not surprised to uncover many of your remarkable achievements. I learned that you are highly respected, kind, and compassionate. I embarked on a detective mission, knowing that understanding more about you would allow me to understand more about myself.

Since then, I have conducted extensive historical research into my Dutch heritage. The events in Rotterdam, the experiences during World War II, and the occupation of the Netherlands by Nazi Germany have left me amazed. My heart tells me that there were many distressing occurrences during that time. There are numerous parallels between that era and my present life that are the link connecting us together.

After much prayer and contemplation, I genuinely believe getting to know you better would be a privilege. My final prayer is that if you are a Christian, you can let go of any fear and see me for the man I am. I humbly request that you allow me to meet with you just once.

It strikes me as ironic that both my wife and I face infertility problems, similar to what you and your wife and my parents experienced. The prospect of having a child of our own appears bleak. However, this circumstance has given me a unique perspective on the bond between fathers and sons and the essence of family.

Now, I yearn for a family of my own and the chance to share both victories and defeats. I firmly believe a life without this joy would be an immense loss. I implore you to reconsider, as I harbor no ill intentions or malice toward you.

Consider, sending this letter to someone who shares genetic code with you and being faced with the

final dagger of silence. More than 30 years later, I am committing this letter to print, for posterity. Whether the donor ever read it or not isn't relevant, since he is long gone now. What matters is that someone will read it, indeed by this point has, and the words lost by a stranger I longed to know will live on past all of us.

PART TWO

The Swan Song

Chapter 19

Truth and Deception Surrounding the Health Freedom Movement: Addressing Vaccine Eugenics

My name is Greg Wyatt, and for those who are unfamiliar, I have been actively sharing my thoughts and ideas for a significant period of time. However, I have reached a point where I am gradually winding down my activities. In the coming months, at the age of 68, I will conclude my mission, reflecting upon its value and moving on. It is rather astonishing to contemplate. The fight against vaccine eugenics can be considered my swan song, and I find the phrase intriguing.

So, what exactly is a swan song? It refers to a person's final public performance or professional engagement before retirement. I have come to the realization that I have done everything within my power to communicate the truth to people in a factual, honest, and understandable manner. However, in today's world, the truth seems to be an unpopular message to convey.

Lies and deception are more readily accepted because the overwhelming cognitive dissonance in our society makes it difficult for people to distinguish between falsehoods and the truth. Nevertheless, throughout my life, I have consistently strived to promote truth and honesty. Admittedly, I am not perfect, but I can honestly say that I have accomplished my goal around 99% of the time. Now, I am facing certain personal matters that I feel compelled to share with you.

Approximately six years ago, I experienced my first seizure. It occurred at 6:00 in the evening while I was watching TV with my loved ones, Joyce, Weston, and Emily. I suddenly felt overwhelmingly fatigued and decided to take a nap. Little did I know that this would be the beginning of a new chapter in my life. By 8:00, I was still asleep, and Joyce woke me up, reminding me that I wouldn't be able to sleep through the night if my nap extended too long. As I sat up, I lost my balance and fell off the bed, disoriented and frightened. This incident raised concerns about what was happening to me and triggered memories of my son's early struggles with walking due to severe dizziness. The cause of his condition is a separate story altogether. After a few days, I started feeling slightly better, but driving became impossible. I felt a constant fear of being in an accident or encountering something dire. Feeling feeble-minded, as if I had Alzheimer's or dementia, was a terrifying experience. Experiencing a malfunctioning brain is perhaps one of the scariest situations one can encounter.

Does anyone recall April 1st, April Fool's Day, 2016? That date holds a special significance for me and many other parents with vaccine-injured children. It was the day the film "VAXXED" was released, a day that forever changed my life. In fact, I even had a customized license plate to commemorate the occasion. I was determined to make a difference by educating people before they made vaccination decisions. These license plates adorned the sides of my car as I drove all over Arizona and hundreds of thousands of people saw them on a weekly basis. As a side note, there was no hostility in the way of people cutting me off or flipping me the bird because of my plates. People seemed receptive to the message and responded to the magnetic messaging that directed them to my effort to assist in raising awareness: AreVaccinesSafe.org.

The film "VAXXED" presented four main premises. Firstly, it aimed to expose the CDC's fraud through the congressional subpoena of William Thompson. We are all familiar with that story, the whistleblower who approached Brian Hooker, with whom I developed a close relationship during the CDC rally. I held deep respect for him and his endeavors. Secondly, the film sought to repeal the 1986 National Vaccine Injury Act, which shields vaccine manufacturers from liability for the harm caused by their products. This act rendered them essentially immune from accountability for the injuries and deaths caused by their hazardous concoctions. Thirdly, the film raised awareness about the link between vaccines and autism, which continues to be a hot topic of debate to this day. Finally, the movie aimed to encourage honest conversations about vaccine safety and the need for more research.

As I watched "VAXXED," my world was rocked to its core with the hope that the movie would bring more exposure to the autism and vaccination connection. My prayer was that "VAXXED" would help get laws changed so children could stop being maimed before they had a chance at life. I had been sharing Weston and Emily's stories for a handful of years before the movie came out to raise awareness of the immense suffering experienced by countless individuals as a result of vaccines. Informed consent should be in place, but is nearly impossible to achieve, since most pharmaceuticals come with pages long warnings and contraindications and doctors that can't be bothered to spend more than fifteen minutes in the room. I came to interpret the informed consent part of the movie messaging as the sick idea that with informed consent, doctors should still be able to poke poison into the veins of children that are too young to consent to the consequences that will plague them for the rest of their lives, ruin their lives, or take their lives. This bait and switch requires many doctors to bully young or uninformed parents into the 'convenience' of skipping normal childhood illnesses like chicken pox so there are no sick days from work or school in the future. That's the reality—and sugarcoating it hasn't worked and will not work.

From that moment onward, I embarked on a journey that encompassed many speeches, discussions, presentations, and collaborations. I dedicated myself to researching, studying, and accumulating knowledge about vaccines and their adverse effects. My goal was not to sway people with emotion but to present them with the factual information of Weston and Emily's story as my focus and allow them to make their own informed decisions. It was a challenge that I embraced wholeheartedly.

However, as the years went by, I began to witness a disconcerting shift in society's attitude towards the truth. The ability to have respectful and open conversations about difficult topics started to erode. People became polarized, entrenched in their beliefs, and less willing to consider alternative perspectives. The advent of social media platforms, while offering unparalleled connectivity, also fostered echo chambers and confirmation bias. It became increasingly difficult to penetrate these digital walls and reach those who held different viewpoints.

But I don't want to dwell on the negative aspects. Despite the challenges, I met countless individuals who shared my commitment to truth and the well-being of others. Their support and encouragement were instrumental in carrying me forward. Together, we organized events, participated in conferences, and made our voices heard. I am immensely grateful for the opportunities I had to connect with like-minded individuals, forming lasting friendships along the way but things were not always they seem.

Now, as I stand on the precipice of retirement, I reflect on the impact I have made. I am proud of the lives I have touched and the seeds of doubt with establishment medicine and vaccinations that I have planted in the minds of those who were open to questioning the status quo. My hope is that these seeds will continue to grow and inspire change in the future.

In conclusion, this swan song is not a lamentation, but a celebration of a life dedicated to truth and the pursuit of a better world. As I step back and transition into a new phase, I do so with gratitude for the experiences, the people, and the lessons I have encountered on this remarkable journey.

Thank you for being a part of it. What follows is a glimpse of what's coming in the second book interwoven with my story of fatherhood, which has surprisingly held an intrinsic parallel to my early life. The ultimate goal is to combat the use of any form of eugenics and the abuse of genetics through the medical model.

Chapter 20

The Bait and Switch of the Movement

It is evident that one would have to live in seclusion not to grasp the current state of affairs. Let's take COVID-19, for instance. They recently discontinued one of the COVID-19 shots due to its link to blood clots. This is not groundbreaking information; we were already aware of it. However, if you were to share such facts on Facebook or social media, you would be permanently removed.

Another issue was the immediate availability of single MMR (measles, mumps, and rubella) shots, which was championed by Andrew Wakefield. He played a significant role in the associated film, and like many others, had financial interests while heralding a safer vaccine that fell in line with his vaccine patents as a vaccine developer. These ulterior motives are widely known. Nevertheless, I assure you, my friends, that I have never had any hidden agenda in this matter, and I will continue speaking the truth until I am unable to do so. Period. It is a fact that Andrew Wakefield held the vaccine patent for the single-shot MMR, and this is not mere speculation.

Another aspect was the classification of vaccines as pharmaceutical drugs, subject to appropriate testing protocols. However, let's be realistic: this will never happen. Can we truly trust the government? For years, I have posed this question to people who entered my shop. Even those working within the government lack trust in it.

Now, let me address the final part. Polly informed me about Del Bigtree and Andrew Wakefield's involvement. I questioned their motives, and as I delved deeper, I was astounded by the truth I uncovered. I used to hold great respect for these individuals, and my entire life revolved around this movement.

However, the unfortunate reality is that the four initiatives they propagated never materialized as they portrayed them. I believe the Autism Trust was established for the benefit of the movie's parents and their close friends. Now, years later, how many people, apart from the lady who donated the land, and their own children, are genuinely residing there? Not one hearing was held and not one law was changed because of the movie, despite its 'goals.' It is essential to ask questions if we are to uncover the answers.

Let me briefly share my personal experience in setting up similar facilities. Most of you are unaware that in 2001, my wife and I purchased a commercial property in downtown Prescott—an old rooming house with 30 rooms zoned for business. Our children, Weston and Emily, were very young at the time. I have always had a heartfelt connection with people with disabilities, influenced by my father and shaping my entire being. We pondered the future of Weston and Emily when they reached 21. This was a question we asked ourselves two decades ago. What would become of them?

I had a friend named Brad Newman who operated similar facilities in Prescott Arizona in the early 90s. Brad was a true humanitarian that founded in his organization in 1974. Today they have over 45 employees assisting over 150 individuals at three training and employment facilities and have expanded into multiple housing complexes, earning countless awards for their contributions to the communities. Unfortunately, due to the severity of Weston's autism he would not be a good candidate for placement at these facilities.

Brad and I discussed the predicament faced by Down Syndrome and Autistic individuals as they grew older. We held meetings, and it became clear that it was a significant challenge. Thus, we proceeded with renovating the entire building, equipping each room with beds, and making it a livable space.

When the time came, I approached Brad and said, "Brad, we are ready." He had spread the word and spoken to some of his residents, informing them about the opportunity to move in. The parents were 20 years ahead of us, feeling worn out by the never-ending struggle. These parents needed respite, as some couldn't handle the situation, and tragically, some passed away, but you learn to just grin and bear it. Where would these children go? Establishing such a facility seemed like a brilliant idea. I had contemplated the same idea long before these individuals. We prepared everything, and we had a couple of prospective residents lined up for the upcoming weekend. I'll never forget that moment; we were excited to take the first step. However, Brad called us and informed us that the parents had backed out. It was a rude awakening.

The reason they changed their minds was that their grown children, despite their age, didn't want to leave. We find ourselves in a similar situation with Weston and Emily. Weston was scheduled to move into a residential home in October, and when the reality was approaching rapidly, we had doubts. It's an ideal situation where he will receive the necessary care, surrounded by highly trained and committed individuals who already know him. Everyone in town who knows someone with autism is familiar with Weston, Emily, and my wife, Joyce, and me. We are respected members of the community, not part of any deceitful group. However, when Joyce looked at me with tears in her eyes, she expressed her belief that she couldn't adequately care for Weston for another ten years. We discussed it further, and the positive aspect is that we can pick him up one weekend per month, bring him to our home or take him wherever we want. Of course, our options are limited due to his deafness and his tendency to vocalize loudly. Starting the day at 6 in the morning, we wake up to Weston with his games blaring, breaking the silence and blaring TV breaking any quiet moments, making peace an elusive concept.

What did Weston Wyatt do to deserve this situation? What did Greg Wyatt and Joyce Wyatt do to deserve their circumstances? Life is unpredictable, my friends. Life is full of unexpected events. Let's go back to 2001 when my wife and I were property investors. We were involved in property flipping in 2003, and at that time, we owned 25 rental units. If we still had those units today, they would be worth millions. However, the rent prices back then were only about 20-30% of what they are now. Unfortunately, due to the educational needs of Weston and Emily, we had to relocate multiple times all over the United States. We built our dream house in Prescott that we couldn't even live in for the first five years because we were constantly chasing education opportunities. This led to additional expenses such as mortgage payments, insurance payments, and frequent airline trips. Then, in 2008, the economy crashed, adding more challenges to our situation.

Now, let's focus on the Marina House. After purchasing it, my wife and I realized that it wouldn't work as originally intended. The parents of the children involved were not willing to give up their kids. To all the new parents out there, you understand the challenges of raising a child with special needs. It's easy for people with good intentions to be taken advantage of in such situations. Throughout my life, I have always lived by the principle of putting God first, others second, and myself last. Imagine if everyone prioritized the happiness of others before their own; we would live in a utopia, like the Garden of Eden.

So what did we decide to do with the Marina House? It became a full-time job for me, and to this day, it accommodates 17 low-income and disabled veterans in downtown Prescott. The cost of living in the area has skyrocketed, resembling a smaller version of Santa Barbara, California. These individuals need a place to live, especially with the presence of the veteran's hospital and the increasing number of disabled veterans affected by the consequences of war, such as Agent Orange exposure. Many of them are in their sixties and seventies, and they share the reality that they have more life behind them than ahead of them. My goal has been to provide safe and secure housing for these veterans by collaborating with various agencies, including Catholic Charities along with other church organizations and Arizona's Veterans' Resources.

Real estate investment has been a significant part of our lives, but when Weston and Emily came into the picture, everything changed. I had a real estate company called America's Home Store and was in the process of franchising. I also owned a company called Leads for Agents LLC, which specialized in building websites and generating leads for real estate brokerages and agents. However, my life took a turn for the worse when my real estate company became infested with mold, leading to my severe illness from 2005 to 2010. This is a part of my story that not many people know. I share these personal details because I realize that my time on this Earth is limited, and it's important to make a difference in the lives of others.

Chapter 21

From Reclusive to a Growing Family:

A Miraculous Journey

I firmly believe that everything is guided by God's hands. Previously, I lived in Weston, Nebraska and was content with staying there indefinitely. However, concerns were raised by my sisters, who feared I might become a recluse due to my tendency to either seek the center of attention or withdraw from crowds entirely. During this time, I went on a blind date—an unexpected turn of events. I met Joyce, a tall blonde woman, at a video store in Columbus, Nebraska, on a cold winter night in December 1994. I walked in, unsure about the situation, but decided to give it a chance. Little did I know that this encounter would be life changing.

Joyce and I became inseparable in the following months, discovering how much we had in common. She was a fascinating and creative person, just like me. We discussed starting a family and potential names for our future children. We considered various Nebraska-inspired names, like Lindsey and Madison. We were captivated by the idea of having a child together, and life seemed to be dealing me winning hands at every turn.

Initially, I had no idea that Joyce was the video store owner where we met, nor was it a crucial detail to me. Money has never been a primary motivator for me. If I were to make money, I wanted it to be through my efforts rather than relying on anyone else's success. My mantra growing up was that setting goals was important. Attaining those goals meant working at them.

After our honeymoon, we received an unexpected check from a major video store conglomerate interested in purchasing all of Joyce's stores. She showed me the amount and asked where I would like us to move. We explored various locations, gravitating towards Arizona due to Joyce's Southwestern roots. Among the places we considered, Prescott stood out the most. The beauty of the area captivated us, and we quickly decided this was the place to be. Within a few days, we were buying a house, and within a week, we found another location for a video store. This store was one of the most profitable ventures ever undertaken. It made me feel like I was contributing something meaningful—a genuine success story in video stores.

While our business thrived, we also pursued our dream of having children. As we had hired employees to manage the video store, it allowed us to explore other avenues. After a couple of back-to-back unsuccessful attempts at in-vitro fertilization, we experienced heartbreak. However, we refused to let our hopes fade away. We decided that adoption was the best path for us. With the help of a private attorney, I meticulously drafted a profile showcasing who we were, what we stood for, and why we would be the perfect parents for an unborn child.

The adoption process was competitive, as only a limited number of unborn children were available for adoption. We found ourselves among approximately 200 families vying for a chance to be chosen. The attorney warned us not to get our hopes up, emphasizing that it could take years or never come to fruition. Undeterred, we patiently awaited news.

Remarkably, within the first month, we received the call. We had been chosen, competing against another couple. Ultimately, the birth mother chose us because we were open to adopting either a boy or a girl, while the other couple had told the birth mother through their attorney that they would only accept a girl. Thus, our journey as parents began with the arrival of our son, Weston. We formed a lasting friendship with the birth parents, cherishing the open adoption experience. However, over the past 20 years, we have lost touch with them. Weston's birth parents were an unmarried teenaged Catholic Hispanic couple, both clean-living and drug-free individuals who had differences but made a selfless decision for their child.

Our joy multiplied when we received another call just 19 months later—an opportunity to adopt again. To our surprise, it was the same birth parents; this time, they were unsure whether they were having a boy or girl until the end of the pregnancy, but they knew we would be happy regardless of the gender. Emily joined our family on New Year's Eve, a year after Weston's birth. Our two little miracles completed our lives, and I couldn't help but feel immensely blessed.

However, there was one hurdle we had to overcome in the adoption process. The paperwork required us to disclose any felony convictions. As an honest and transparent person, I revealed my past to Joyce, fully expecting her to distance herself from me. This included my involvement in eugenics, sterilization, and my concerns about government activities. To increase our chances of adoption, I had to clear my record. Joyce took charge and guided me through the process. It involved scheduling meetings with the secretaries of state, attorney general, and state prosecutor in Nebraska. I appeared before a tribunal where my record was scrutinized. I had to face intense questioning, knowing that clearing my past sins was necessary for us to adopt Weston.

Chapter 22

Bound by Love, Shattered by Vaccines

The reality of the adoption process hit us hard. We were informed that due to the prevalence of abortions, there would be a three to four-year waiting period since many mothers chose to bypass motherhood and opt for terminating unwanted pregnancies. The demand for adoption far exceeded the available children, with a ratio of 20 hopeful parents for every non-existent child.

Drawing from my experience in sales and marketing, I crafted a compelling profile to increase our chances of being chosen. Surprisingly, our efforts paid off, and less than a month later, we received the life-changing news. Our profile struck a chord with an expecting couple, and we were selected to become parents.

Over the following months, we built a close bond with the birth parents, fully embracing the concept of open adoption. We needed to establish a connection and ensure that the journey ahead would be one rooted in trust and mutual understanding. Both children, born healthy and happy, brought immense joy to our lives. They possessed a blend of Hispanic, Filipino, and American Indian heritage, a perfect match that added to the beauty of our diverse family.

Monitoring the birth mother's pregnancy became a shared responsibility. We eagerly watched her stomach grow larger each month, feeling a mix of anticipation and awe. Cassandra, the birth mother, and Alex, the birth father, were young individuals— only 16 and 18 years old. Some may have questioned their readiness for parenthood, but as we stood in the delivery room, witnessing our son Weston entering the world on Groundhog's Day in 1998, any doubts dissipated.

The initial medical advice was straightforward—Weston only needed the Hepatitis B and vitamin K shots. However, within hours, jaundice  cast a yellow hue over his tiny body, prompting the doctors to recommend circumcision when he was just ten days old. We followed their guidance, believing it was in our child's best interest.

Little did we know that Weston's two-month well-baby visit would mark a turning point. Despite our reservations, we succumbed to pressure from a young, affable doctor who belittled us for expressing concerns about vaccination. Each subsequent visit, at four and six months, resulted in a similar experience. Weston would fall ill, and the doctor would dismiss it as a normal part of childhood, prescribing antibiotics alongside Tylenol and Motrin, to be administered around the clock.

As weeks passed, Weston's health deteriorated, and a multitude of unexplained ailments plagued him.

It became clear that each round of vaccinations had gradually transformed him into a victim of vaccine injury. Yet, the progression was subtle and elusive, especially for two inexperienced parents enraptured by their newborn. Weston's once joyous and healthy demeanor swiftly vanished, replaced by persistent sickness and an ever-growing list of doctor visits.

Dr. Mick contacted us again over one year later, recommending the MMR vaccine. Fast forward to today, and Weston remains a twenty-five-year-old trapped in a body that functions at the level of a three- to four-year-old. His life, a creation of God, had been disrupted and forever altered by the malevolent forces of vaccination, an insidious satanic ritual.

The aftermath of Weston's vaccine injury impacted our family and my business. Parents would enter, seeking guidance, and I would share Weston and Emily's vaccine injury story. As the years went by, I noticed a startling revelation. Contrary to the CDC's claim that 90% of children were vaccinated, less than 50% of my clients' children had received vaccinations. The children that had received none were thriving, while the children that had received vaccinations had histories of chronic illness, ranging from earaches and stomach issues to more serious issues. The lies began to unravel, layer by layer, as I delved deeper into the truth, becoming increasingly educated about the dangers surrounding vaccines. And that brings me to where I stand today.

Weston is now twenty-five, at the writing of this book, yet his developmental progress mirrors that of a three- to four-year-old child. Emily, his younger sister, has made some strides, functioning at the level of a nine- or ten-year-old. Although my children are God's most precious gifts bestowed upon me, the journey of caring for them presents an ongoing challenge—one I wouldn't wish upon anyone. Each morning I awaken, and every night before bed, I find strength in persevering and giving my utmost, guided by the faith God has instilled in me.

Life has a way of surprising us, even when we think we've prepared for every possible outcome. Weston and Emily's presence is a constant reminder of the profound impact that unforeseen circumstances can have, shaping their lives and those around them. And so, with determination and love, we continue to navigate this extraordinary path, embracing the unwavering commitment to provide the best for our children, despite our adversities.

Chapter 23

Weston's Autism Journey:

A Doctor's Reassurance, Lingering Doubts

Weston and Emily were adopted 19 months apart, with Weston being the first to join the family on Groundhog's Day, February 2nd, 1998. On the other hand, Emily was born on September 14th, 1999. Remarkably, they share the same birth parents. Both infants were delivered at Phoenix General Hospital in Phoenix, Arizona when their birth parents were very young.

Weston, weighing a perfect 6 pounds and 8 ounces, entered the world without complications. I vividly remember that day, as if it were yesterday, watching his tiny head emerge from the birth canal. It was a sight I had never witnessed before, making me feel a bit queasy.

I saw Weston's birth mother and his precious head as I entered the room. Suddenly, I heard the cries of a newborn baby, and at that moment, I knew that my life had changed forever.

It was hard to believe that at 43 and 41, Joyce and I finally obtained the right to become parents after all those years of waiting. Tears streamed down our faces as we hugged each other in a long embrace, realizing that our lives would never be the same as they were the day before.

Due to receiving the hepatitis B injection, Weston had to stay in the hospital for two additional days. During that time, he was diagnosed with arrhythmia and experienced toxicity throughout his body. Shortly after, he developed jaundice and required an oxygen tent and an IV. He remained in the hospital for several days until he was finally healthy enough to go home.

We were overjoyed to bring our new baby home. He symbolized hope and filled our hearts with happiness and optimism.

To ensure we provided the best care, we meticulously kept a diary, noting Weston's sleep patterns, feeding times, and every detail of his routine. We were determined to do everything perfectly!

Weston's first visit to the pediatrician was with Dr. Mick, which was a pleasant and uneventful experience.

We wanted to ensure we were doing everything right, but it surprised me when the doctor's secretary scheduled Weston's next appointment only two months later. I questioned the timing, wondering why such a healthy baby needed to be seen so soon. Nevertheless, she swiftly booked his following three appointments consecutively. Two months later, all three of us, Joyce, Weston, and I entered the examination room, where Dr. Mick greeted us and

138

promptly placed Weston on the scale. He documented Weston's weight, measured his head, and prepared a tray of needles for the vaccinations.

At two months old, Weston received his first set of injections, which included the DTaP vaccine for Diphtheria, Tetanus, Pertussis, Polio, and Hib. This vaccine combination was designed to "protect him from various and dangerous childhood illnesses."

On that significant day, Weston received a total of seven different vaccinations, all aimed at "safeguarding him from potentially life-threatening diseases." Unfortunately, we were unaware at the time that vaccines could cause harm, especially since we were denied informed consent and nothing was disclosed or explained to us. Like so many other autism parents have found out the hard way, as we try to follow the "professionals" and their "science," the 'innocent' nature of vaccinations is a game of Russian Roulette. Some children will seem unscathed, their autoimmune disorders blamed on genetics, while others will have life altering effects, while still others will lose their lives and might be deemed SIDS cases. Ignorantly, we subjected our son to significant injury that would impact him for the rest of his life.

When I expressed my concerns to the doctor about the necessity of such vaccinations, he assured

139

me that they were vital for Weston's well-being and the development of all children. Like most parents, we trusted his expertise, as he was a medical professional, and we were not. This "trust" relationship doesn't work out when the doctors lie, hide, or are ignorant of life-altering information. Hiding the side effects doesn't take them away, and there was no disclosure of the dangers of vaccines. We were refused informed consent without knowing the medical oversight was going to change the course of our lives. Sadly, over the following days, we observed subtle and gradual changes in our once cheerful and angelic baby.

He became irritable, distressed, clearly having stomach pain. Weston had received three shots of five different vaccines during that visit, and another appointment was scheduled for two months later to repeat the procedures. This time, Weston cried even more. He suffered from colic and stomach discomfort, exhibiting unusual behavior such as vomiting and trembling. Dr. Mick assured us that everything was fine, but Weston's condition continued to worsen.

One of my favorite activities was sitting and gazing at Weston, admiring his beautiful brown eyes, thick hair, and perfectly formed ears, cherishing the

miracles of life. I loved placing my nose against his cheek and inhaling deeply, reveling in the unique scent of a baby. For those who haven't experienced it, there are no words to truly describe it.

Eventually, my wife contacted Dr. Mick again as Weston's health did not improve. We made another appointment to express our concerns, only to be told that kids get sick all the time, implying it was a normal part of childhood. The damage had already been done, but the changes were subtle and gradual, unfolding over days, weeks, and months. Weston's well-being continued to deteriorate. He was born perfectly healthy, but within hours of receiving the hepatitis B injection, he fell gravely ill and was diagnosed with multiple illnesses. After six months, the routine well-baby visits ended, but our journey of endless doctor's appointments had just begun. Something was profoundly wrong with Weston, and his condition was far from right.

By September 28th, 1998, approximately ten months later, Weston was chronically unwell. We sought medical attention as he had a persistent cough and wheezing, struggled to breathe, and fought to survive. He experienced severe congestion, projectile vomiting, liquid diarrhea, a high fever of 104 degrees, and incessant crying that lasted for several days. Merely looking at the DTaP vaccine insert revealed that Weston had exhibited symptoms of various illnesses listed there. He was diagnosed with bronchitis and prescribed albuterol, in addition to being instructed to alternate Tylenol and Motrin every four hours. At this point, Weston had been unwell for several months.

Weston displayed distressing symptoms such as coughing, vomiting, head-banging, and projectile vomiting. His diarrhea emitted a toxic electrical smell.

141

Less than a month later, on October 23rd, we took Weston to the doctor, demanding answers about his deteriorating health. He had been sick for several months by that point. Weston exhibited cold symptoms, a low-grade fever, wheezing, and continuous vomiting throughout the night. The doctor prescribed more albuterol and advised us to continue alternating between Tylenol and Motrin every four hours. Additionally, Robitussin DM was added to the treatment regimen, along with prednisone steroids.

By November 3rd, 1998, Weston's condition had worsened significantly, and he remained gravely ill. We visited the doctor again, where Weston weighed 21.6 pounds at nine months old. His weight gain had been minimal or nonexistent over the past few months. He was constantly sick, experiencing severe vomiting, respiratory distress, and wheezing. Nonstop breathing treatments with Albuterol and steroid shots were  administered, but his respiratory rate remained in the sixties, accompanied by audible wheezing and evident respiratory distress.

On November 4th, several weeks later, we returned to the doctor and received a diagnosis of reactive airway disease, an upper viral respiratory infection with bronchospasm. Weston's treatment included more steroids, albuterol treatments, and cough syrup. The doctor suggested hospitalization if his condition did not improve.

On the 16th, twelve days later, Weston had his twelfth doctor visit within a little over nine months. He continued to cough and wheeze incessantly, as if something were lodged in his throat, persisting day and night. The coughing had intensified, occurring around a hundred times per hour. In addition, he began vomiting two to three times every hour. The prescribed treatment remained albuterol, Tylenol, and Motrin, administered round the clock.

Two weeks later, we visited the doctor again, discovering that Weston had lost five pounds from his already too small frame. His coughing had become nonstop, occurring several hundred times an hour. These records clearly documented his condition. Weston's vomiting was almost continuous, and we were advised to induce vomiting to clear the mucus so that he could find brief moments of sleep. His health had spiraled out of control, presenting severe congestion and emesis restrictive airway disease. His lungs sounded like those of a heavy smoker of fifty years. We continued the albuterol three times a week, along with breathing treatments as needed, which turned out to be two to three times per hour. More steroids were prescribed.

During this period, Weston continued missing his developmental milestones. He didn't start walking until he was 18.5 months old, around the time Emily came home from the hospital, due to persistent dizziness that affected his balance. Classic symptoms of autism were evident, although no one

143

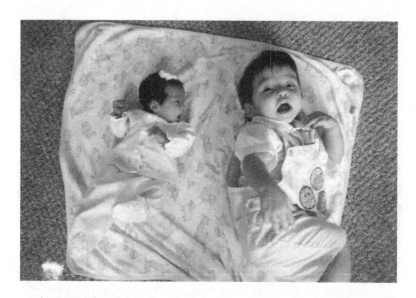

acknowledged it. Until the age of one, Weston hadn't walked at all, but rather moved around on his knees. We referred to him as a "knee walker." Looking back, it became apparent that his dizziness prevented him from standing on his feet for prolonged periods, prompting him to resort to walking on his knees. There were times he would hang onto furniture for prolonged periods of time to keep himself from falling. He grew easily frustrated and continuously banged his head. Discomfort led him to remove all his clothes, including shoes and socks, as they made him feel incredibly uneasy. We couldn't comprehend the reason behind his actions, nor could he. His screaming escalated gradually until it reached a point of constant, all-night high-pitched shrill screams. Projectile vomiting and foul-smelling diarrhea became even more severe. It was an unbearable ordeal for our entire family. This was a time when we should have been enjoying our precious son, Weston.

You know what dealing with all of this medical intervention with worsening symptoms with your children causes? It causes PTSD - Post-Traumatic Stress Disorder. Only the millions and hundreds of millions of parents who have experienced vaccine injuries can truly understand what I'm talking about. It affects not only your children's minds but also your own. I remember coming home from work, leaving early in the morning and returning around six or seven in the evening. I would go to the garage and reach for a bottle of whiskey to ease the pain. One drink would provide some relief, so I would take another, hoping to alleviate more pain. After three or four drinks, which became my nightly routine, I was done. It helped calm my nerves. My wife, busy with the kids, didn't drink at all.

Then, there was a time when I went to the dentist and was prescribed pain pills. Taking a couple of pain pills made my pain go away. The relief was miraculous, a pharmaceutical miracle. I went to refill the prescription and did it again. This was back in 2000, 2001, when online pharmacies were available. It was as easy as making a phone call or going online to get Vicodin, which was the popular one, available in 5mg, 7.5mg, or 10 mg doses. I went from taking one or two Vicodin a day to two to four a day.

Fueling my work with this coping mechanism eliminated the pain and made everything seem better, at least temporarily. I thought to myself that I was only 47 years old at the time (around 2002), and I could continue this for a couple more years just to manage. I used these pills to cope while existing every day, but I wasn't truly living.

Despite my success in business, owning a real estate brokerage firm, and my drive to provide for my children, there was no joy or happiness left. It felt like the essence of life had been drained away, and I could see it in my wife's face. Joyce is an incredible wife and mother, a pillar of strength who never gives up or gives in. My beautiful wife, Joyce, is happiest when she is helping others, an attribute I greatly admire, and one that began rubbing off on me.

She's the rock while I'm the one filled with emotions. I kept working, setting lofty goals, becoming the number one online real estate agent in 2004, recognized by my peers for lead generation. I was like Zillow before Zillow even existed, like Redfin before Redfin was ever thought of. All I wanted was to create a legacy for my kids because it seemed unlikely that Weston would ever fully recover.

Now, my entire life seems to have flown by in an instant, and I'm left as a 68-year-old man with many past successes but also a lot of baggage created through the monetization of misery imposed by our medical community upon ourselves and humanity. I rarely thought about it before because it was too painful, but did they deliberately do this? I'll never forget the day I came to the realization that, yes, they did. I say this with all my heart: my friends, I am deeply sorry. So much beauty in the world has been stolen, taken away unjustly. It's absolute nonsense.

Chapter 24

Emily's Diagnosis:

Balancing Businesses and Babies

When Emily came, she became the new focal point of our growing family. Given our busy schedules and business commitments, we made the decision to hire a full-time nanny. In 1999, our video business was flourishing, making more money in a month than the average person made in a year. Additionally, the food storage business I had started from scratch was also thriving, easily surpassing those figures. At the time, it seemed like our success was boundless, and my confidence in my sales and marketing skills convinced me that I could venture into any new business and achieve remarkable results. However, I was cautious about not disclosing the exact amount of money we were making, as success often attracts its own challenges.

Emily entered our lives, just as perfect as Weston had been in our small family of three. Our family grew to four, but little did we know of the dangers that were ahead.

Following the recommended schedule, we vaccinated both Weston and Emily during their well visits at two, four, and six months of age. We were oblivious to the underlying issues with Weston, and it was only later that we discovered the vaccines had played a role in his condition.

Emily was a delightful addition to our family, and with the success of my businesses and Joyce's joy in having her little girl, I found myself somewhat detached from the severity of Weston's challenges. Unlike Weston, I didn't experience any chronic illnesses and seemed to be relatively healthy. Looking back, it's apparent that the vaccines were administered differently, some stronger than 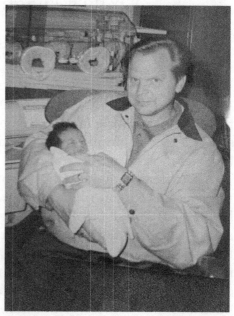 others, without the intention of creating a widespread epidemic of infant sickness. This made it difficult to pinpoint the exact cause. Some children made it through relatively unscathed, while others suffered more. Emily fell somewhere in the middle.

Once Weston was diagnosed with autism at the age of three, the pieces of the puzzle began to fall into place. We made the decision not to vaccinate Emily again, knowing that the damage had already been done. However, it would take some time for us to comprehend the true extent of the situation. The malevolence behind these actions is unfathomable, and it continues unabated without any consequences.

At the age of five, we took Emily for testing. The results indicated that she displayed some possible symptoms of autism, but the diagnosis wasn't

148

definitive. I vividly recall the professional telling us that it was a 50/50 chance she had autism. As it turned out, she did have it.

Joyce and I discussed the pros and cons of officially diagnosing Emily with autism. Joyce was hesitant because she didn't want her to share the same diagnosis as her brother. However, we recognized that a formal diagnosis would open doors to services and assistance in undoing the damage caused and addressing the challenges. Ultimately, we decided that Emily should receive the diagnosis.

This situation was a severe blow, transforming my life from one of happiness to one of darker despair.

There is a systematic approach to handling cases like ours. Once you enter the system, they offer early intervention programs through the government-sponsored education system, which is entangled in a web of lies and deception. They make you believe that you're doing your child a great favor, when in reality, it's all part of the malevolent scheme. They call it

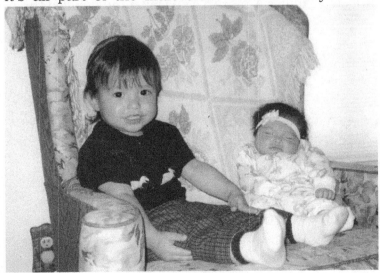

"early intervention," a lucrative enterprise. Weston became a part of it from an early stage, while Emily seemed to fare better and didn't require it, at least we didn't think so at that time. Emily didn't start kindergarten until she was seven, and as she grew older, the developmental gaps became more evident, indicating that something was amiss.

After completing his early intervention program, Weston officially entered the public school system. On his first day of school, Joyce visited and discovered a chaotic scene with a dozen children crammed into one room, accompanied by only two aides. She promptly withdrew him from that environment, marking the beginning of a twelve-year struggle to find suitable education not only for Weston but also for Emily.

The stark difference between Weston and Emily and the decision to vaccinate Emily despite Weston's unknown injury becomes a crucial point of discussion. It is important to note that we had canceled Emily's 4-month well visits and delayed them

to 6 months. Even then, we decided to cancel the 6-month visit as well, but unfortunately, the MMR vaccine was administered at the very end. The details surrounding these events are deeply distressing and may shed light on why Emily's condition is categorized as moderate while Weston's is severe, as every child is affected differently.

Emily, now 23 years old, possesses the spirit of an 8-year-old and enjoys indulging in pasta and vegetables. Her journey began perfectly until her 2-month well visit, which proved to be a turning point. By opting to delay and cancel subsequent well visits, we unknowingly made a crucial decision that may have saved her life. However, the persuasion of medical professionals led us to proceed with the MMR vaccination on May 14th, 2001. As a result, Emily now lives with mild to moderate autism, while Weston's condition is far more severe.

Both Emily and Weston require round-the-clock care and supervision for the entirety of their lives. The tragedy they face is not isolated, as countless others share similar stories due to the darkness that has pervaded our world. In my solemn promise to God, I vowed to share Weston and Emily's story as long as I breathe, with the hope that it may save others from experiencing a similar fate. Their tale serves as a reminder of the importance of awareness and understanding, and the urgent need to protect and support those who face similar challenges.

152

Chapter 25

Amidst the Inferno:
Chasing Education

I was sitting in my office on that fateful day, June 18th, 2002, when the phone call came, piercing through the tranquility of the afternoon. It was my wife on the other end, her voice trembling with fear and urgency. She relayed the news that our subdivision was being evacuated due to an unprecedented fire that was ravaging Arizona. At that time, the Rodeo-Chediski Fire was the largest fire recorded in the United States, burning 468,638 acres over the many days it took to get the fire under control. Panic and concern welled up within me as I listened to her describe the fiery red glow outside our home, with gentle ashes falling from the sky like silent whispers of destruction.

"Greg, you have to come home right away," she pleaded, her voice choked with tears. At that time, our son Weston was four years old, and his severe autism presented immense challenges. Our daughter Emily was approaching her third birthday, adding to the weight on Joyce's shoulders. While I sought solace in my work, building my financial empire and supporting our family, the chaos at home grew. It became a daily routine for me to arrive home after 6:00 PM, slipping into the garage to numb my nerves with a couple of shots of Jack Daniels. But then, a dental surgery led me to discover the numbing comfort of pain pills, which gradually replaced my reliance on alcohol. I entered a cycle of addiction, seeking refuge from the emotional torment that accompanied our children's condition.

Despite the struggles we faced, life continued, and our financial endeavors thrived. My emergency food storage business, established in 1998, seemed to turn everything it touched into gold. We decided to move back to Prescott, leaving our countryside dwelling in Dewey, Arizona, to be closer to civilization. We purchased a house in the serene Hidden Valley Ranch subdivision, nestled among tall pines. From an outsider's perspective, my life seemed idyllic, complete with financial success and material abundance. However, the escalating challenges posed by Weston's autism and the growing concerns about Emily's development cast a shadow over our seemingly perfect existence.

As Weston attended the public school system for early intervention, Emily's vaccinations were halted as we noticed signs of something amiss in her development. Each day, we focused on maintaining a positive attitude and clinging to hope for positive outcomes, even as the weight of uncertainty pressed upon us.

Financially, we were thriving. My ventures in emergency food storage and the video store consistently generated substantial income, with days where I made tens of thousands of dollars. We owned properties across multiple locations, including a home in Rapid City, South Dakota, and a self-sufficient Y2K compound in Pine Flat, Arizona. In addition to a condo on Lake Biltmore in Phoenix, we also had rental properties sprinkled through our area that brought in additional income. The illusion of unchanging prosperity led me to believe that my talent for making money would never falter.

However, the devastating fire we experienced shattered that illusion. Determined to prevent our children from enduring such a traumatic event again, we made the decision to leave our beloved home and subdivision behind. In its place, we embarked on the arduous journey of building a custom home specifically designed to accommodate the unique needs of our two autistic children. The process involved meticulous planning and construction, and in 2004, our new home stood proudly as a symbol of our unwavering dedication to our children's well-being. We had ensured that we used only the best, the paint and carpet were VOC and chemical free. We poured over information to make sure everything was environmentally safe. The backyard was like an amusement park, so to speak, with a circular path that extended around the 2/3-acre lot so Weston and Emily could ride their scooters and bikes without us needing to be concerned about traffic.

We moved into our new abode during the Christmas weekend of 2003, enveloped by a sense of energy and excitement. Gratitude overflowed from within me as I woke up each morning, tears streaming down my face, acknowledging the blessings bestowed upon us. Yet, amidst the joy, we still lacked answers concerning our children's conditions.

Weston completed preschool in May of 2004, and we enrolled him in the special education program offered by the Prescott Unified School District. However, our hopes were quickly dashed on his first day. The classroom was chaotic, with only a handful of students and ill-prepared aides. It became clear that Weston would not receive the education he needed in that environment. Frustrated and determined to advocate for our son, we threatened the school with a lawsuit and sought an alternative.

Our search led us to Play ABA, an autism school in Tempe, owned by Tara Rice, renowned for her expertise and highly trained staff. To ensure Weston received the education he deserved, we embarked on a grueling 200-mile daily round trip from Prescott to Tempe. The toll became too much to bear, and we ultimately purchased a home in Glendale, Arizona, to ease the burden of the journey. However, even with the new residence, the hours spent commuting left us in a state of limbo, passing hours upon hours at malls and restaurants until Weston's school day concluded. We clung to the weekends, returning to our vacant Prescott home, juggling two mortgage payments and the associated expenses.

After negotiating with the Prescott Unified School District, they agreed to fund another year of Weston's education at Play ABA, granting us a reprieve from the relentless travel. The financial burden was substantial, with each child's education costing $26,400 per year, paid directly to the school in Tempe. Sadly, throughout the negotiation process, it was clear that our special needs children were not wanted in their district. Their inability to work with us in a way that we felt comfortable and confident that the children would thrive caused a lot of heartache and despair.

Two years into our exhausting routine, the exhaustion consumed us. The never-ending pursuit of education had taken its toll, and we knew we couldn't sustain this grueling pace indefinitely. The time had come to make a profound decision that would shape our future.

Considering options within Arizona, we explored cities like Yuma and Lake Havasu but found them lacking in the educational opportunities we sought. Expanding our search nationwide, we turned our attention to the Midwest, familiar with its different outlook on special education and a proactive stance towards supporting families like ours.

Flying to Missouri, we embarked on a comprehensive tour of major and minor cities, including Springfield and Columbia. Our exploration yielded no satisfactory solution until we arrived in Columbia, Missouri.

Columbia stood out with its exceptional focus on special education, boasting the prestigious University of Missouri and a highly regarded program for children with special needs. As we stepped into the classrooms, a sense of amazement washed over us. The programs were meticulously organized, the staff remarkably trained, and love and care permeated the air—a perfect fit for Weston and Emily.

Uncertainty lingered in my mind as I grappled with the decision to leave Arizona, a place where we had established our lives over nearly two decades. The Midwest's harsh weather extremes—searing heat, bitter cold, and treacherous ice—added to my doubts. Yet, a gentle voice whispered within me, urging me to delve deeper into Columbia. I shared this revelation with Joyce, and we turned the car around, retracing our steps to Columbia for further investigation before finalizing our decision.

Those subsequent days spent in Columbia solidified our choice. It was time to uproot our lives, bidding farewell to Arizona and embracing the promise of a fresh start.

Chapter 26

Losing Weston:
The Reality of Letting Go

In 2020, the news reached us: Weston's school had unveiled plans to construct a home designed for severely and profoundly autistic boys who had grown into adulthood. The announcement struck a chord with us, for it reminded us of a time fifteen years prior, in 2008 when Joyce and I participated in a local TV show. The show focused on the looming question that haunted every parent's mind: What will become of our children when we are no longer here to care for them?

This concern was especially poignant for parents of autistic and special needs individuals. As time passes and we grow older, our physical strength wanes while our children, in their twenties, grow more robust and capable. The weight of the future rested heavily upon our shoulders as each passing day turned into months and years, gradually transforming into decades of unrelenting stress, fear, worry, and anxiety.

Autism, it seems, had a way of unraveling the life we had envisioned, tearing it apart from the way God had intended. It had already shattered our dreams for our beloved son, Weston, and the man he could have become. As the years went by, it became increasingly clear that certain milestones would forever remain out of his reach. He will never submit a job application, get behind the wheel of a car, never partake in sports, and never achieve the level of independence we had hoped for. The list of things he will never do extends far beyond what I am willing to contemplate.

It was easier to push these difficult decisions aside in the earlier years, deferring them to an uncertain future. But eventually, reality caught up with us, and we were forced to confront the truth of our circumstances. We had fought tirelessly to provide Weston with the best educational opportunities, pouring hundreds of thousands of dollars into various supports and services.

When Weston was eight, we received the heartbreaking news that he was rapidly losing his hearing. It was likely that he would eventually become completely deaf. To mitigate the impact, he was fitted with hearing aids, presenting new challenges and obstacles. The discomfort of having foreign objects lodged in his ears led him to repeatedly yank them out and throw them away. We would spend hours searching for them, only to train him continually to keep them in place. It was an ongoing battle, but as the years passed, it became less hostile and easier to manage.

We took the initiative to teach Weston sign language, persisting with his reading and writing lessons despite his severe disabilities. Today, he exists in a world devoid of sound, with silence as his constant companion.

In the early years, we could avoid thinking about the possibility of Weston leaving the only family he had ever known. Yet, September of 2022 loomed ever closer as the home we'd chosen for him was coming to completion, a stark reminder of the inevitable. The date was pushed back to October, then November, prolonging our time together as a family. Eventually, December arrived, and a new resident would move into the facility each week, facilitating a smoother transition for the staff. We attempted to delay the inevitable for as long as possible, and Weston was the final individual to relocate, entering the new home in December.

It was the holiday season, and unknowingly, those festivities would mark our last moments together as a family. Weston's departure was delayed by a couple of days, and on January 5th, 2023, he bid us farewell.

That day is etched into my memory, an indelible mark upon my soul.

Despite our extensive conversations throughout the years, acknowledging the possibility that this day might come, we never truly comprehended that we would wake up one morning to find it a haunting reality. We realized then that even the most well-conceived plans may only partially come to fruition.

Chapter 27

A Time for Everything Under the Sun: A Journey Through Deterioration

Losing my health and losing my mind— these once-distant concerns have now become my stark reality. My body and mind, like fading stars, are spiraling into a dark abyss, and I find myself helplessly witnessing the rapid deterioration of my physical and mental being.

Stress, that silent predator, has stealthily invaded every aspect of my life, chipping away at my mind, body, and soul. Days turned into months, and months into years, as the damage slowly manifested itself in insidious ways.

At 68-years-old, my once agile and muscular body is now merely a shadow of its former self—resembling that of someone decades older. Simultaneously, my thoughts and cognitive coherence are slipping through my fingers, and even simple tasks have become increasingly challenging.

As my body and mind crumbled, I sought answers and underwent a series of tests and evaluations. A preliminary diagnosis suggested the possibility of Alzheimer's/dementia. The news shook me to my core, and I was prescribed medication intended to slow down the symptoms.

However, it only left me feeling worse, and I abandoned the medications in search of alternative paths to healing.

The journey led me to Barrow Neurological Institute in Phoenix, where countless others with similar symptoms filled the halls. The stress and uncertainty consumed me, potentially exacerbating the symptoms. Doctors proposed a shunt surgery to drain excessive spinal fluid as a potential remedy, but the decision weighed heavily on my mind.

Throughout the months of extensive testing, I faced a spinal tap, revealing nearly normal pressure. The search for answers continued, accompanied by symptoms like urinary incontinence and walking difficulties.

Finally, the day arrived when the test results were ready. With bated breath, I sat with the head neurologist, awaiting the verdict. Unexpectedly, the Alzheimer's summary test score showed a mere one out of ten, leaving the shunt surgery in doubt.

While grappling with my health battles, we were also preparing for our son Weston to leave our home of 25 years. Life's intricacies and challenges converged, making every day a test of fortitude. The turmoil of the impending diagnoses and Weston leaving intensified my emotions and wore out my coping mechanisms. There was never a plan for Weston to leave us, not knowing the amount of attention and care he needed with his autism. But ecclesiastically, there is a time for everything, and he needs more than I am capable of giving. Plus, having been older parents, the unspoken truth that our children would outlive us became glaringly obvious in the face of my medical issues. Making plans for Weston's future was the only responsible and loving thing to do— even if it meant him leaving to acclimate to his new home and life before we're gone. At least we get to see him thriving and adjusting, still spending time with him on a monthly basis. While these plans were waylaid for several years, the pain of planning was simultaneous with the worst possible diagnoses, which exacerbated the mental anguish of loss.

In 2017, cranial numbness was the initial warning sign, but it soon spread, enveloping my face, thighs, legs, feet, and hands in neuropathy's grasp. Walking unaided became increasingly arduous, and daily tasks turned into daunting feats.

Through it all, I am profoundly grateful for the unwavering support and love of my wife, Joyce. She has stood by my side, a beacon of strength and resilience, as I navigate the uncharted waters of deteriorating health.

As I reflect on the journey of my life, I find solace in the words of the Ecclesiastes 3:1-8:

> 1 For everything there is a season,
> and a time for every matter under heaven:
> 2 a time to be born, and a time to die;

a time to plant, and a time to pluck up what is planted;
3 a time to kill, and a time to heal;
a time to break down, and a time to build up;
4 a time to weep, and a time to laugh;
a time to mourn, and a time to dance;
5 a time to cast away stones, and a time to gather stones together;
a time to embrace, and a time to refrain from embracing;
6 a time to seek, and a time to lose;
a time to keep, and a time to cast away;
7 a time to tear, and a time to sew;
a time to keep silence, and a time to speak;
8 a time to love, and a time to hate;
a time for war, and a time for peace.

While the road ahead remains uncertain, I know that my experiences have brought me to a profound understanding of love, perseverance, and the fragility of life.

And so, my story continues—one of challenges and triumphs, of love and resilience, and of embracing each moment, regardless of the darkness that shadows our paths. In the end, the love and strength shared with Joyce, our children, and loved ones becomes the guiding light through the darkest of times. And as I face the unknown, I will do so with courage and gratitude, cherishing every memory and the life that has been my own.

Epilogue

Embracing the Journey:
Finding Light in the Darkness

A good book is supposed to have a happy ending. Or at least, that's what I was taught to believe. But sometimes, despite our best efforts, life doesn't unfold as we plan. My chronic illness journey has stretched over 15 years, leading me to seek help from various doctors and healing modalities. There were moments of incredible progress, followed by setbacks that left me feeling defeated. The weight of self-blame always lingers, no matter how hard I try to shake it off. Throughout my life, I carried a constant sense of guilt, believing I was never good enough and unable to achieve my goals, no matter how much I struggled or how much I succeeded. As the years went by, it became increasingly difficult to bear.

Here I was, on the morning of my 68th birthday, my mind racing through the faded pages of my life. It was my first birthday in a quarter century without my precious son, Weston, by my side. Time had become the measure of my declining health, and this past year has been the most brutal of all. Despite my prayers for miraculous healing, it seems like the walls were closing in around me. Perhaps age has caught up with me, and my story was meant to come full circle back into my father's embrace.

I wondered if I would ever get better, as each day became more challenging, yet I was aware that each day was a precious gift to endure. The realization that all good things come to an end pushed me to set pen to paper to preserve the horrifying truths that the government and other nefarious players would much rather have buried with those of us that have heralded the truth.

One of my reasons for writing is hoping to stall the eugenics movement that has morphed many times and has continued full speed ahead. Creating mass infertility and reaching diminutive population goals spurs the movement at full speed ahead, and we have seen the "unsinkable" ship when it travels without caution and full of faux pride that it could never fail. Ask the Titanic how the best laid plans sufficed.

In this world, nothing lasts forever, and the journey that had carried me to this point, though difficult and often unbearable, has been filled with experiences and blessings beyond measure. But I had no idea it would end like this. Still, realizations wash over me—I know deep down that it isn't over yet. There is still much work to be done.

My health has been gradually declining for almost 18 years now. In some years, the changes were so subtle that I barely noticed, while other years brought radical shifts that couldn't be ignored. I often wonder if the constant stress and anxiety I have endured throughout my life played a significant role in my declining health. Perhaps it was the culprit for it all.

Observing my elderly friends, who are significantly older than me, surpassing me in vitality and mental strength, fills me with mixed emotions. While I am genuinely happy for them, the added weight of Weston's absence and the drastic changes in my life become more and more depressing with each passing day.

Thoughts of Weston consume me throughout the day. I ponder whether he thinks of me, just as I constantly think of him. His severe autism means his mind doesn't process and recall information like most people's. He is always laser-focused on his electronics, books, food, and favorite movies and shows like *Teletubbies*, *Disney's Frozen*, and *Tangled*. His frequent and obsessive trips to Goodwill in search of new books were his way of finding comfort in the world. He always searches for the same books, even though he already has dozens of copies. It seems like he has committed to buying them all.

Does he miss me, as I miss him? The pain of longing for his presence often becomes overwhelming. I keep his favorite blue shirt on my bed, where I now spend most of my time. Frequently, I lift it to my nose, close my eyes, and imagine he is here with me. It brings solace amid mental turmoil, even if only for a fleeting moment.

I am primarily homebound, and my wife has become my primary caregiver. The thought of venturing into crowded places or driving on busy streets no longer holds any appeal. The cognitive decline, that began with my first seizure over seven years ago, has turned my once vibrant mind into a mere shell of its former self. But I remain determined to never give up, to keep moving forward as best I can, sharing my knowledge and experiences with the world until I can no longer do so.

Ironically, my father, Herbert Wyatt, had been placed in a home for feeble-minded youth in his earlier years. Now, I contemplate the possibility of one day residing in a nursing home, surrounded by others in a similar state of mind. Yet, it is okay. I have lived a remarkable life and understand that nothing in this world lasts forever.

Life comes full circle, and planning our journeys with the end in mind is crucial so we're never disappointed. This book is meant to carry the torch, continue the journey I embarked upon so long ago. This beacon of light in the darkness gets to live beyond me, and I get to say goodbye, which is something not everyone gets the chance to do.

A special thank you to you, the reader. Thank you for allowing me to share the truth, as ugly as it may be. The truth is necessary if real changes are to be made, and they must, in haste, if the human race is to be preserved outside of the eugenicist agenda. Headlines have already boasted of "designer babies," "genetic/gender selection of fetuses in IVF," among so many other nefarious plots that are now readily available if one but pays attention to the jargon and enters the search terms into a web browser. There is no excuse for ignorance when there is so much knowledge available at our fingertips.

My final request, whether I am still living when you pick up this book, or whether I have passed, is that you take up the charge and become a light in the darkness.

To my dearest Weston,

I know that deep inside the recesses of your mind you can hear everything I say even though you are now deaf, and I know that you can understand me also, you just can't articulate back.

You have been my light in the darkness and have touched not only my life but many many others also.

You are the epitome of God himself and that God intended for humanity to be.

You are so kind and gentle with such a beautiful soul. So caring, so charismatic, and affectionate.

You are so focused and committed—looking for your next puzzle, shopping at thrift stores, and your love for life and our family.

I know someday I will see you made whole and restored to what God intended and we will live forever in eternity as father and son. Thank you, Weston, for enriching my life in ways I never could have imagined.

 You will always be my boy— little boy that I waited for all my life!

In loving memory of Herbert Wyatt

Herbert Wyatt, you were a man of unparalleled strength and towering stature, crafted by the very hands of God Himself. Your presence in my life has left an indescribable impact, shaping me in ways beyond measure. In many ways, you embodied the essence of a modern-day Jesus Christ.

You endured immense suffering, yet never uttered a single bitter word against those who caused you pain. Your unwavering resilience was matched only by the eternal smile that graced your face, concealing the hidden tears that welled within your eyes.

When God fashioned the mold for a man like you, known affectionately as "Shorty" Wyatt, it was clear that only one could exist. He then shattered that mold, ensuring your uniqueness would endure for all eternity. To have the privilege of calling you Dad is a blessing beyond words.

Forever in our hearts,

Your loving family

In loving memory of Betty Wyatt

Betty Wyatt, my mother, was a true pioneer in countless ways, but her most remarkable achievement was her unwavering determination in the face of infertility challenges that ultimately led to my birth. She possessed an unyielding focus when she set her sights on something, refusing to give up or give in. Defeat was a concept she simply did not comprehend. It is through her boundless love, understanding, and unwavering support that I have become the person I am today.

Throughout my journey to find the missing pieces of my life, my mother stood by my side, providing unwavering support and encouragement at every step. Even in the darkest of times, she found a way to overcome obstacles with a radiant smile on her face. Though she has been gone for 28 years now, her spirit continues to resonate deeply within my soul. Mom, I love you with all my heart, and I hold onto the belief that one day we will be reunited.

With eternal love,

Your son, Gregory

Weston says, "Wait a moment, turn the page for the suggested reading list before you go.

Suggested Reading List:

- *The Bible.* Your Preference.
- *The Beast.* Jack T. Chick. 1966.
- *Endgame: The Hidden Agenda 21.* Vernon Coleman. 2021.
- *A Stolen Life.* Marge Grant. 2005.
- *The Truth About Polio, Smallpox, Vaccines and Viruses.* Jim Dandy O'Kelly. 2023
- *The Surgical Solution: A History of Involuntary Sterilization in the United States.* Professor Philip Reilly. 1991.
- *Nazi Nexus: America's Corporate Connections to Hitler's Holocaust.* Edwin Black. 2009.
- *IBM and the Holocaust: The Strategic Alliance Between Nazi Germany and America's Most Powerful Corporation-Expanded Edition.* Edwin Black. 2012.
- *War Against the Weak: Eugenics and America's Campaign to Create a Master Race, Expanded Edition.* Edwin Black. 2012.
- *The Belarus Secret.* John J. Loftus. 1982.
- *Where Did the Towers Go? Evidence of Directed Free-energy Technology on 9/11.* Judy Wood and Eric Larsen. 2010.
- *TRANCE Formation of America: True life story of a mind control slave.* Cathy O'Brien and Mark Phillips. 1995.
- *Confessions of an Economic Hit Man, 3rd Edition.* John Perkins. 2023
- *The Creature from Jekyll Island: A Second Look at the Federal Reserve.* G. Edward Griffin. 2010.

- *The Secrets of the Federal Reserve.* Eustace Mullins. 2021.
- *Murder by Injection: The Story of the Medical Conspiracy Against America.* Eustace Clarence Mullins. 2016.
- *America's Nazi Secret: An Insider's History.* John Loftus. 2010.
- *Behold a Pale Horse.* Milton William Cooper. 1991.
- *The Poisoned Needle: Suppressed Facts About Vaccinations.* Eleanor McBean. 2021.
- *Margaret Sanger: Father of Modern Society.* Elasah Drogin. 1989.

Through illness, we find health.

Through forgiveness, we find peace.

Through adversity, we find strength.

Thanks for reading!

-Greg Wyatt

Made in United States
Orlando, FL
06 August 2023

35835895R00104